Spirit
TOUCHING
Spirit

A CONTEMPORARY HYMNAL

COMPILED BY
HANDT HANSON

PRINCE OF PEACE PUBLISHING
Burnsville, Minnesota 55337

SPIRIT TOUCHING SPIRIT

Introduction for Contemporary Worship Book

This book is the result of 12 years of work with contemporary worship at Prince of Peace Lutheran Church in Burnsville, Mn. In that time we have seen the joyful response of our people as we use language and music consistent with our culture to tell the Good News that we know so well. It is my hope that these hymns and worship settings might open new doors for you and your congregation.

Special thanks needs to be said to the people involved with Summer-Song, our contemporary worship leading group — for their part in how this music and ministry has grown and evolved over the years. I also need to thank Henry Wiens for his hard work in writing arrangements for each and every hymn in this book.

We have tried to be sensitive to the varieties of needs that surround us today. We have tried to be inclusive in our language usage as much as possible. For instance, we do not use male pronouns when we speak of God or the Holy Spirit but when we speak of Jesus. We have not, however, changed the male pronouns in the creeds, scripture songs, or when speaking of the Father, Son, and Holy Spirit. We have tried to paint accurate word pictures that can communicate the Good News of the Gospel of Jesus in new ways.

The piano arrangement and guitar chords for each song are meant to be a guide to begin playing the songs. To reach their full potential, the songs need a full rhythm section and strong vocal leadership. I would encourage you to experiment with your worship settings and to be creative in the musical leadership so that worship can be as meaningful as possible to as broad a cross-section of worshipper as possible.

Handt Hanson

TABLE OF CONTENTS

Spirit Touching Spirit

Music and Lyrics by Handt Hanson
© 1985 Prince of Peace Publishing. Used by Permission

That Kind of Love

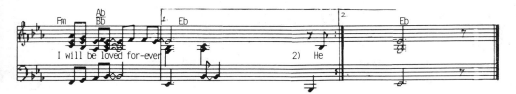

I will be loved for-ever   2) He

He looks for me when I try to hide- He comforts me when I cry
He rescues me when I drift away-He holds me close when I feel all alone
His love is like that- His love is like that

Chorus

Music and Lyrics by Handt Hanson
© 1985 Prince of Peace Publishing. Used by Permission

Come Touch

Come touch His heal-ing hands come
touch His wounded side and feel the love that waits like a
bridegroom for the bride come touch His healing hands come
touch His wounded side and feel the love that's giv-ing
broken hearts new life Out-stretched arms wai--ting for you--
love's em-------brace a--------------lways Come

Music and Lyrics by Handt Hanson
© 1985 Prince of Peace Publishing. Used by Permission

Go and Do

Music and Lyrics by Handt Hanson
© 1985 Prince of Peace Publishing. Used by Permission

We Who Believe

Once Again

VERSE 2) We will offer-grateful praises-once again-and worship Him
We'll surrender heavy burdens-once again- and worship Him

Music and Lyrics by Handt Hanson
© 1985 Prince of Peace Publishing. Used by Permission

Psalm 105

Music and Lyrics by Paul Murakami
© 1985 Prince of Peace Publishing. Used by Permission

Paul's Song

VERSE 2) I don't give everything to the needy
I don't deliver my body for burning
I don't have all the faith to move the mountains high
Without love- without love I am nothing

Music and Lyrics by Handt Hanson

Rest in My Love

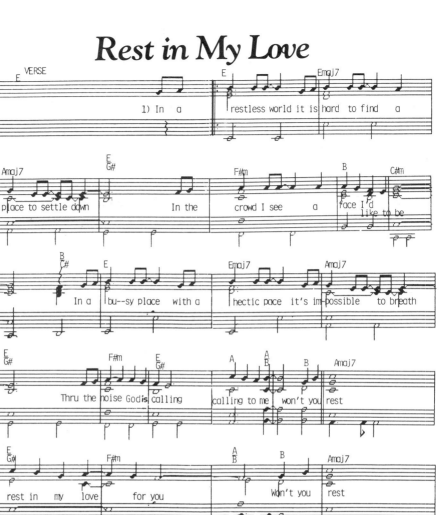

1) In a restless world it is hard to find a place to settle down In the crowd I see a face I'd like to be In a bu--sy place with a hectic pace it's im-possible to breath

Thru the noise God is calling calling to me won't you rest rest in my love for you Won't you rest rest in my hand and you'll see

see what I'll do through you If you believe on-ly believe that I can 2)Never

VERSE 2) Never slowing down - always spinning round
A step behind the pace
In the mirror stands a stranger with my face
After nine to five- I feel half alive
Success a distant race
Through the noise God is calling-calling to me

Music by Handt Hanson, Lyrics by Handt Hanson and Steve Swanson
© 1985 by Prince of Peace Publishing. Used by Permission

A Prayer for You

10

VERSE 2) Give them blissful peace without despair
Give them life and health and things to share
Give them blessings way beyond compare
Give them love- give them love

Music and Lyrics by Handt Hanson
© 1985 Prince of Peace Publishing. Used by Permission

Where Two or Three Gather

12

Doxology

Psalm 20

Music and Lyrics by Handt Hanson

What a Difference You've Made in My Life

Words and Music by
ARCHIE P. JORDAN

1+3) What a dif'rence you've made in my life What a
change you have made in my heart What a

dif'rence you've made in my life You're my sun------shine day and
change you have made in my heart You've re- -placed all the bro-----------ken

night Oh, what a difference you've made
parts Oh, what a change you have made

in my— life
in my life

What a heart

Love to me was just a word in a song that had

been way o-----ver used but now I've joined in the singing 'cause you've shown me love's true meaning that's why I want to spread the news 1) What a life

The Shadow of the Cross

VERSE 2) The garden is cold tonight-my friends are out there sleeping
This cup I'll have to drink alone is bitter from the memory
VERSE 3) The cross is cold tonight- the crown I wear is bleeding
My sin weighted shoulders ache- My heart is barely beating

Music and Lyrics by Handt Hanson
© 1985 Prince of Peace Publishing. Used by Permission

We Can Be Lifted Up

VERSE 2) When confusion seems the standard condition
And nothing's making sense anymore
When the only thing you're doing is nothing
You'll know the time has come- to look up
toward the Son

Music and Lyrics by Handt Hanson
© 1985 Prince of Peace Publishing. Used by Permission

Welcome to the Family of Love

VERSE 2) This is the time for remember'ring
The faces of the ones who love you
And with your promise saying
You will love them too
This is the time to acknowledge
This perfect love is not our doing
Our God is here and giving
Love our whole life through

Music and Lyrics by Handt Hanson
© 1985 Prince of Peace Publishing. Used by Permission.

Christ Is Alive

Music and Lyrics by Handt Hanson
© 1985 Prince of Peace Publishing. Used by Permission

I Want to Be Like Jesus

Je----sus   Je-sus

VERSE 2) In everything I think- In everything I want
        I want to be like Jesus
        To think about the best- and pray about the rest
        I want to be like Jesus
VERSE 3) In everything I am- In everything I'll be
        I want to be like Jesus
        To be my very best and pray about the rest
        I want to be like Jesus

Music and Lyrics by Handt Hanson
© 1985 Prince of Peace Publishing. Used by Permission

Psalm 36

VERSE 2) Your constant love is deeper than the oceans
        Your shelter is the shadow of your wings
        Your feast of life is flowing like a river
        How precious is your love-your constant love
        God of great power and might.

Music by Handt Hanson and Lyrics Paraphrased Scripture
© 1985 Prince of Peace Publishing. Used by Permission

Sing a New Song

VERSE 2) When you face each new temptation-sing a new song
When everything is going wrong just- sing a new song

Music and Lyrics by Handt Hanson
© 1985 Prince of Peace Publishing. Used by Permission

Hands and Knees

22

Music and Lyrics by Handt Hanson and Paul Murakami
© 1985 Prince of Peace Publishing. Used by Permission

Soon and Very Soon

Words and Music by
ANDRAÉ CROUCH

VERSE 2) No more crying there   VERSE 3) No more dying there

Let Us Break Bread Together

Traditional Spiritual

Let us break bread to-gether on our knees

Let us break bread to-gether on our knees

When I fall on my knees with my face to the ri-sing sun Oh Lord have

mercy on me

2)Let us drink wine together 3)Let us bow round the altar
4)Let us praise God together

God Is So Good

25

African Melody

God is so good God is so good God is so good He's so good to me

VERSE 2) He cares for me
3) I'll do His will
4) He loves me so
5) God answers prayer

Wake Up

VERSE 2) There's a new sun rising, breaking through
Lighting up the darkness cov'ring you
There's a new sun rising, there's a new sun rising

Music and Lyrics by Handt Hanson
© 1985 Prince of Peace Publishing. Used by Permission

Praise the Lord

Words and Music by
BROWN BANNISTER and MIKE HUDSON

Our Father

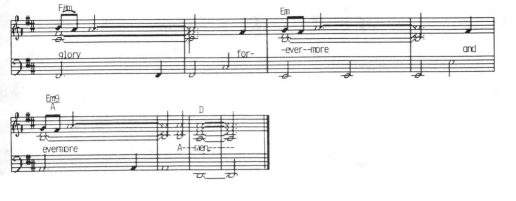

glory   for-   -ever--more   and

evermore   A--men---

Hear Us

Hear us   we're your children   and we   need a word of hope to-----day

Feed us   with your vision   Give us   comfort as you hear   our   prayer

give us   strength to face today   calm   our   fear   as we   pray

Hear us   we're your children   and we   need a word of hope to--day   Hear us

He Brings Peace

INTRO Em Emsus2/D C6 B7sus B7

VERSE Em Emsus2/D C6 B7sus B7

What can a baby do   in this world   It seems so out   of   control

Em Emsus2/D C6 B7 CHORUS C D

What can this tiny ba--by of God   bring to a world dark and cold   He brings

G Bm Em Am D

peace   He brings love   He brings   hope to a world in need   He brings peace

Bm Em Am C/D

He brings love   He brings   vi-------------ctory   and His

Em G/F C/E Cm/A

hope   calms our   fear   and His   love   ne--ver ends   He brings

G/D C/D 1. G F#7 B7

peace,   love   hope and   victory

2. G C/G G/D C/D

He brings   peace   love   hope and   victory

VERSE 2

What can this child alone in this world
Do to correct what is wrong
God in our flesh became one of us
If we believe we will know

Music and Lyrics by Handt Hanson
© 1985 Prince of Peace Publishing. Used by Permission

Go in Peace and Serve the Lord   31

Music and Lyrics by Handt Hanson
© 1985 Prince of Peace Publishing. Used by Permission

One Free Gift

VERSE 2
I've seen what God's love can do in believers
The difference it makes for me is going to last forever
And when I stumble God is always there to take my by the hand

Music and Lyrics by Handt Hanson and Paul Murakami
© 1985 Prince of Peace Publishing. Used by Permission

All Day Song

33

Words and Music by
JOHN FISHER

Love Him in the mornin' when you
And in the in-between times when you
see the sun ar------isin'
feel the pressure comin'

Love Him in the evenin' 'cause He
Remember that He loves you and He
took you thru the day
promises------to-stay

Fine

When you think you have to worry

'Cause it seems the thing to do

Remember He's not in a hur-- ----ry He's

always got time for you

D.C. al Fine

The Spirit Moved Me

VERSE 2) When we look back and remember- we can see the purpose
The changes we've been through have led the way to you
And we will follow
We are in the world not of it- we will rise above it
The enemy is strong-the battle may be long
But we will follow- we will follow

Music and Lyrics by Handt Hanson and Paul Murakami
© 1985 Prince of Peace Publishing. Used by Permission

I'll Belong to You

I'll be- long to you for- -e----------ver I'll belong to you for- -e----------ver Je-sus take me as I am take me by the hand and I'll belong to you

(3rd x Fine)

VERSE 1)Many are the roads we'll tra--vel many are the times we'll fall away

Help me to recall your promise Help me to believe ev'ry day

VERSE 2) Many times we'll be in trouble
Many times I'll come to you and say
Help me to recall your promise
Help me to believe everyday

Music and Lyrics by Handt Hanson
© 1985 Prince of Peace Publishing. Used by Permission

Come Closer

36

VERSE 2) If your heart won't stop hurting
Feel like giving up
There's a Savior who's giving
Life on a cross with all His love

Music and Lyrics by Handt Hanson
© 1985 Prince of Peace Publishing. Used by Permission

O Strength

VERSE 2) O life- O glory- O Prince of Peace
O joy- O Savior- O Mighty Grace
My suffering friend- My sheltering home
My Spirit's need

Music and Lyrics by Handt Hanson and Paul Murakami
© 1985 Prince of Peace Publishing. Used by Permission

Joyful, Joyful, We Adore Thee

HENRY VAN DYKE
Arr. from Ludwig Van Beethoven

VERSE 2) All Thy works with Joy surround Thee,
Earth and heav'n reflect Thy rays
Stars and angels sing around Thee
Center of unbroken praise
Field and forest, vale and mountain
Flow'ry meadow-flashing sea
Chanting bird and flowing fountain
Call us to rejoice in Thee

VERSE 3) Thou art giving and forgiving
Ever blessing - ever blest
Wellspring of the joy of living
Ocean depth of happy rest
Thou our Father, Christ our Brother,
All who live in love are Thine
Teach us how to love each other
Lift us to the joy divine

VERSE 4) Mortals, join the mighty chorus
Which the morning stars began
God in love is reigning o'er us
Jesus' love binds heart and hand
Ever singing, march we onward
Victors in the midst of strife
Joyful music lifts us sunward
In the triumph song of life

Psalm 27

The Lord is my light and my sal-vation I will never be a-fraid The Lord protects me from all danger I will never be a-fraid When e-----vil at-tacks and tries to kill me I will never be a-fraid E------ven if whole ar----mies surround me I will never be a-fraid

-fraid 2) In -fraid I will never be afraid

VERSE 2) In times of trouble He gives shelter- I will never be afraid
God will keep me from all danger-I will never be afraid
He prepares the path before me- I will never be afraid
I will live to see God's glory- I will never be afraid

Music and Lyrics by Handt Hanson
© 1985 Prince of Peace Publishing. Used by Permission

Victory

40

He rose up from the grave with pow-er to save Sal-vation for every-

-one The angel rolled away - the stone on that day- victory has been

won! He victory has been won! victory has been

won! victory has been won

Music and Lyrics by Handt Hanson
© 1985 Prince of Peace Publishing. Used by Permission

Take Me, Lord

41

Take me, Lord I give to you Ev---'ry---thing and all I do my

love, my life is my of----fering that I give to you

RIT.

Music and Lyrics by Handt Hanson
© 1985 Prince of Peace Publishing. Used by Permission

Jesus Is Born

42

VERSE 2) Born a savior- in a manger- born to save from sin
Holy, Holy Lord almighty-born to save from sin

VERSE 3) Come and join our celebration- Christ is born today
Hallelujah, our Messiah- celebrate and sing

Music and Lyrics by Handt Hanson and Paul Murakami
© 1985 Prince of Peace Publishing. Used by Permission

Go—Make Disciples

43

Music and Lyrics by Handt Hanson
© 1985 Prince of Peace Publishing. Used by Permission.

To Him Who by the Pow'r

Words: Parphrase of Ephesians 3 by JOHN YLVISAKER
Music: JOHN YLVISAKER

44

To Him who by the power within is able to do more than we can to

Him be glory without end A-men A---men

We Give Ourselves to You

45

Fa---ther in heaven we thank-you For all the blessings you give

You are the source of our po---wer You are the reason we live

Help us to constantly fol---low and keep our eyes on you

Fa-ther with daily commit---ment we give ourselves to you

Music and Lyrics by Paul Murakami

We Are the Reason

Words and Music by
DAVID MEECE

Broken in Love

47

Music and Lyrics by Handt Hanson

I Can See His Face

Psalm 3

49

VERSE 2) Lord, please let me do your will—make your way plain
Save me from my enemies— and hear my voice

The Lord Bless You and Keep You

Words and Music by
PETER C. LUTKN

We Love You

VERSE 2
Now we've said it once it once again
We've opened up to you
We know you love to hear from your children
We never want to stop-saying this to you
We want the world to hear
These words we have for you

Music and Lyrics by Handt Hanson
© 1985 Prince of Peace Publishing. Used by Permission

Alleluia

JERRY SINCLAIR

2)Blessed Jesus   3)My Redeemer

Lord, Be Glorified

Words and Music by
BOB KILPATRICK

VERSE 2) In my song Lord, be glorified, be glorified
In my song Lord, be glorified today

VERSE 3) In Your church Lord, be glorified, be glorified
In Your church Lord, be glorified today

Give Him Praise

VERSE 2) Give Him- love He deserves
Give Him- grateful adoration
And as you do- give Him praise- give Him praise

Music and Lyrics by Handt Hanson
© 1985 Prince of Peace Publishing. Used by Permission

Cup of Love—Bread of Life

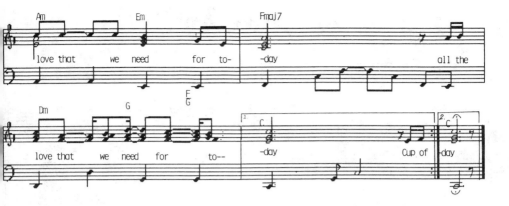

Music and Lyrics by Handt Hanson
© 1985 Prince of Peace Publishing. Used by Permission

Make Us One

56

Music and Lyrics by Handt Hanson
© 1985 Prince of Peace Publishing. Used by Permission

Doxology

Traditional Words by Thomas Ken
New Music by JIMMY OWENS

Praise God from whom all

bles------sings flow praise Him all cre------atures

here be-----low Praise Him a-----bove the

hea-----ven---ly host praise Fa----------ther, Son, and

Ho----------ly Ghost

Christ Is Risen

Music and Lyrics by Handt Hanson
© 1985 Prince of Peace Publishing. Used by Permission

Easter Song

Words and Music by
ANNE HERRING

Hear the bells ringing they're singing that we can be born a--gain
Hear the bells ringing they're singing "Christ is risen from the dead"

The an---gel up on the tombstone said "He is ri---sen just as He said Quickly now Go tell his disciples that Je-sus Christ is no longer dead" Joy to the world He is ri---sen Al--e---lu--ia he's ri----sen Al--le-lu----ia he's ri----sen Al---le-------------lu-----ia

Father, I Adore You

Words and Music by
TERRYE COELHO

Fa-----------ther I ad--ore you Lay my life be-----fore you How I love you

VERSE 2) Jesus
3) Spirit

For Me

The Greatest of These Is Love

VERSE
1) All the beauty of the earth can----not compare with love All the riches of the world can-----not compare with love Even faith to move mountains, or hope for each val-ley can--not compare with this. I love we share The

CHORUS
greatest of these is love more than anything you can think of The greatest of these is love more than faith and hope and every gift love sent the Savior to show what love will do and this

love is why I give my---self to you | you

VERSE 2) All the things that we possess
cannot compare with love
All the dreams we hope to see
cannot compare with love
Even faith to move mountains or
hope for each valley cannot compare
with the love we share

Music and Lyrics by Handt Hanson
© 1985 Prince of Peace Publishing. Used by Permission

Benediction

May the grace of the Lord and the love of our God and the fellowship of the

Spirit be with you Lord Jesus Christ give you peace every---day and His un-dying love

light from above lead your way

Music and Lyrics by Handt Hanson
© 1985 Prince of Peace Publishing. Used by Permission

Communion Song

Words and Music by
BARRY McGUIRE

Take this bread I give to you and as you do re---mem-ber me This bread is my body broken just for you take it eat it each time you do re---member me re-member me me re-member me re-member me

VERSE 2) Take this cup I fill for you
And as you do remember me
This cup is the new covenant
I'm making with you
Take it, drink it, each time you do
Remember me

VERSE 3) Take this love I've given you
And as you do, remember me

Psalm 5

65

VERSE 2)

I can sleep in peace forever- I'll not be fearful alone
My God protects me
In the night and in the daytime- I'm not afraid
I'm at home   My God has blessed me

Music by Handt Hanson and Lyrics Paraphrased Scripture
© 1985 Prince of Peace Publishing. Used by Permission

Good Things

Come to Me Today

VERSE 2) I know your sinning- I feel your hurting
I want to make you new again
Your search is over- I'm your Creator
I will change your life today

Color Me

VERSE 2)   Brown for the ground beneath my feet
            Yellow for the light of day
            Green for the things that grow
            I'm one of your children- color me one

VERSE 4)   Brown for the things we do together
            Yellow when you make me smile
            Green growing more like you
            I'm one of your children-color me one

Music and Lyrics by Handt Hanson and Paul Murakami
© 1985 Prince of Peace Publishing. Used by Permission

I Am the Promise

Peace 70

Hold On

VERSE 2) Forty days and nights for Noah- hold on - hold on
There's a rainbow promise for you- hold on- hold on
Daylight coming- with the dawning
Daylight coming- hold on- hold on

VERSE 3) Hear the word for Moses children- hold on- hold on
Trust the Lord for your deliverance- hold on- hold on
Freedom coming- with the morning-
Freedom coming- hold on- hold on

Music and Lyrics by Handt Hanson

I Wonder If He Knew

VERSE 2) In the shadows of the stable light
Came this tiny flame's beginning
From the darkness of that humble place
Came light to illumine every heart

VERSE 3) From the moment of that lowly birth
All the world is somehow different
Out of Christmas and this time of love
The gift of new life is giv'n through Him

Music and Lyrics by Handt Hanson
© 1985 Prince of Peace Publishing. Used by Permission.

Leave Your Heart With Me

Music and Lyrics by Handt Hanson
© 1985 Prince of Peace Publishing. Used by Permission

Jesus Is the Answer

Words and Music by
ANDRAÉ CROUCH and SANDRA CROUCH

Psalm 9

Music by Handt Hanson and Lyrics Paraphrased Scripture
© 1985 Prince of Peace Publishing. Used by Permission

Thank You for the Gift

Music and Lyrics by Handt Hanson

O Come, Let us Adore Him

77

From Cantus Diversi

O come let us a---- dore Him O come let us a--- -dore Him O come let us a-- -dore Him---- Christ------- the

Lord

2)For He alone is worthy
3)For Jesus is our Savior
4)We kneel in adoration
5)O Praise Him, alleluia

Mary Had a Baby

78

Words: Traditional American
Music: Traditional American

Mary had a baby   my Lord   Mary had a baby   my Lord

Mary had a baby   Mary had a baby   Mary had a baby   my Lord

2) What did she name Him?
3) She named Him King Jesus
4) Where was he born?
5) Born in a manger
6) Angels were singing
7) Glory, hallelujah!

The Promise of Love

Music and Lyrics by Handt Hanson
© 1985 Prince of Peace Publishing. Used by Permission

Psalm 8

VERSE 2) You have made us just less than only you
And crowned us with glory and honor
And appointed us over all things too
Your greatness is everywhere

Music by Handt Hanson and Lyrics Paraphrased Scripture
© 1985 Prince of Peace Publishing. Used by Permission

I Am Sure

Lord, Listen to Your Children

Music and Lyrics by Handt Hanson
© 1985 Prince of Peace Publishing. Used by Permission.

In Love for Me

Words and Music by
JIMMY OWENS

INTRO Eb / Ab/Eb / Eb / Ab/Eb

Ebmaj7 / Ab/Eb / Ebmaj7 / Ab/Eb

This is my bo---dy   bro-ken   for you

Ebmaj7 / Ab/Eb / Db / Bb7

bring-ing you   wholeness   ma---king you   free

Fm7 / Bb7 / Gm / Cm

take it and   eat it   and when you   do

Fm7 / Fm7/Bb / Bb7 / Ebmaj7 / Ab/Eb

do   it in   love   for   me

Promise Me a Rainbow

VERSE 2) Been so long with the night surrounding,
haunting, hiding— what we do
Been so long— then your love reclaimed us, healed
us— brought us— back to you

Music and Lyrics by Handt Hanson and Paul Murakami
© 1985 Prince of Peace Publishing. Used by Permission

Spiritborne

86

Music and Lyrics by Handt Hanson
© 1985 Prince of Peace Publishing. Used by Permission

Jesus, Jesus

Je--------------------sus, beau-tiful Sa--------------------vior
love live in me--------------------
Je--------------------sus precious re--de--------------------emer
Cross set me free--------------------
Je--------------------sus Je--------------------sus
Take all of me

Music and Lyrics by Handt Hanson
© 1985 Prince of Peace Publishing. Used by Permission

Go Out in Power

Music and Lyrics by Handt Hanson
© 1985 Prince of Peace Publishing. Used by Permission

This Is the Day

Music and Lyrics by Handt Hanson
© 1985 Prince of Peace Publishing. Used by Permission

I Don't Belong to Me

Music and Lyrics by Handt Hanson

Lord, Make Me an Instrument

Rise and Sing

Music and Lyrics by Handt Hanson
© 1985 Prince of Peace Publishing. Used by Permission

Don't Be Anxious

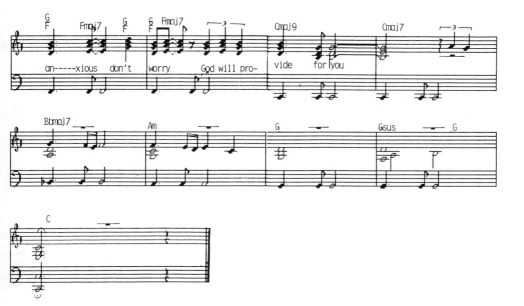

an-----xious   don't   worry   God will pro-   vide   for you

VERSE   2) God give to the birds of the air- food and drink
                 for the season
            God gives to the flowers in the field- sun and
                 and rain when it's needed
            What will we eat- what will we wear
            If God loves them do you think that He cares for you

Music by Handt Hanson and Lyrics Paraphrased Scripture
© 1985 Prince of Peace Publishing. Used by Permission

Psalm 23

Celebrate His Supper

Music and Lyrics by Handt Hanson
© 1985 Prince of Peace Publishing. Used by Permission

Prepare the Way of the Lord

Pre- -pare the way of the Lord tell everybody about Him Pre-

pare the way of the Lord tell everybody He's coming

shout for joy Je---ru--salem Shout for joy you nations of God

Jesus is coming to save the world Pre- -pare Him a place in your heart Pre

pare the way of the Lord

Pre- Lord

Music and Lyrics by Handt Hanson
© 1985 Prince of Peace Publishing. Used by Permission

Don't Hide It–Shine It

shine it   shine it

Holy, Holy

98

Ho----ly O ho------ly Lord most High

God of po---wer and might   The heavens declare your ma-jesty   Ho-

-sa----na to God most High   Blessed is He who comes in the name of the

Lord   Ho---sa--------nna   O   Ho--ly O ho-ly Lord most High   Ho-

-sa-nna to God most High   O   High

Life in His Hands

Music and Lyrics by Handt Hanson
© 1985 Prince of Peace Publishing. Used by Permission

Waterlife

1. Be-fore I can_ re-mem-ber_ the
2. A sim-ple sweet be-gin-ning_ a
3. My hope and ex - pect-a - tion _ for

cov-en-ant was sealed With Fa-ther, Son and Spi-rit_ In wa-ter was re-vealed The
lov-ing place to start_ _ God be-gan the sing-ing_ that swells with-in my heart His
true com-mun - i - ty_ Be-gins with re - sur-rect-ion_ His death and life in me His

cleans-ing was for cer tain_with wa-ter and the word Gen-tle words were spo-ken_ In
love be-came my call-ing_ His life my min - i-stry His name is my_ a-dopt-ion_ in-
spi-rit fills the bo-dy_ His church thru wa-ter sees Prom-ise for to-mor-row_ His

heav-en they were heard ___ They were sing-ing wa - ter-life be-gin-ning life_
to His fam - i - ly__
Wa-ter-life in me_

Wa - ter-life All _ my life Wa - ter-life Spir-

1. It life _ Wa-ter-life   **2.** Wa-ter-life

Music and Lyrics by Handt Hanson
© 1985 Prince of Peace Publishing. Used by Permission

God Himself Is Here

101

Music and Lyrics by Handt Hanson
© 1985 Prince of Peace Publishing. Used by Permission

He Just Sees Jesus

Oh What Joy

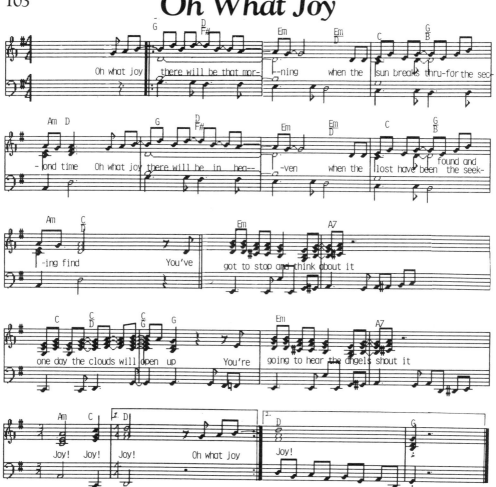

Music and Lyrics by Handt Hanson
© 1985 Prince of Peace Publishing. Used by Permission

Good Soil

Lord, let my heart be good soil open to the seed of your word Lord let my heart be good soil Where love can grow under-stood When my heart is hard break the stone away When my heart is cold warm it with the day When my heart is lost lead me on your way Lord, let my heart Lord, let my heart Lord, let my heart be good soil

Music and Lyrics by Handt Hanson
© 1985 Prince of Peace Publishing. Used by Permission

The Building Block

Words and Music by
NOEL PAUL STOOKEY

VERSE 2)   There is a man, who has collected
All the sorrows in our eyes.
He gives us love, as God directed,
but is seldom recognized

VERSE 3)   When all your dreams, have been connected,
and your vision has been returned.
Remember, love, you are protected,
by the truth your heart has learned.

We Are His People

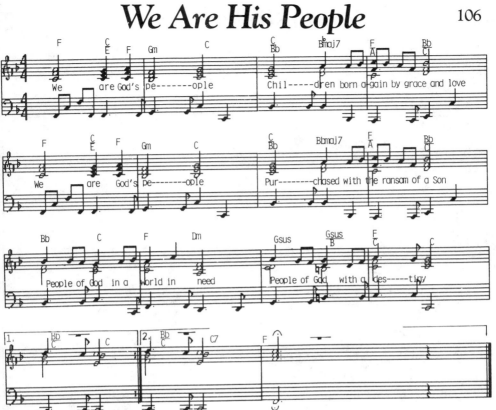

Music and Lyrics by Handt Hanson
© 1985 Prince of Peace Publishing. Used by Permission

Hallelujah

Words and Music by
SHANON SMITH

VERSES 2 and 4) Hallelujah, you have made us what we are
by your blood and by your scars
We want to praise You in every way we can

Make Me Like You

Words and Music by
JIMMY and CAROL OWENS

108

Lord make me like you please make me like you

You are a servant Make me one too O Lord I am

willing Do what you must do to make me like you Lord, Just

make me like you

Amazing Grace

109

JOHN NEWTON

A-maz----ing grace how sweet the sound that saved a wretch like me I

once------ was lost but now----------I am found, Was blind but now I

see

VERSE 2) 'Twas grace that taught my heart to fear
And grace my fears relieved,
How precious did that grace appear
The hour I first believed

VERSE 3) Thru many dangers, toils and snares,
I have already com
'Tis grace hath brought me safe thus far
And grace will lead me home.

VERSE 4) When we've been there ten thousand years,
Bright shining as the sun
We've no less days to sing God's praise
Than when we first begun

Come to Me

Words and Music by
JOHN YLVISAKER

VERSE 2)

Come to me, through the mystery,
I'm a refugee from the torment of the soul
Jesus hear my plea, in Gethsemane,
Quickly come to me-make me whole

Celebrate Love

VERSE 2) We can sing about His love for us
Jesus loves everyone
He is living here inside of us
Jesus loves everyone

Music and Lyrics by Handt Hanson
© 1985 Prince of Peace Publishing. Used by Permission

Hear Our Prayer

Hear our prayer Lord, in this mo - ment Here we pray o - pen, for-giv - en Hear our prayer Teach us to lis - ten Here is our life Do what You will.

Music and Lyrics by Handt Hanson
© 1985 Prince of Peace Publishing. Used by Permission

I Want to Tell His Story

113

Music and Lyrics by Handt Hanson and Paul Murakami
© 1985 Prince of Peace Publishing. Used by Permission

I Love You, Lord

Words and Music by
LAURIE KLEIN

I love you Lord and I lift my voice To wor---ship You, O my soul re--joice Take joy, my King in----- what you hear May it be a sweet, sweet sound in Your ear

Mary's Little Boy Child

Words and Music by
JESTER HAIRSTON

VERSE 2) While shepherds watched their flocks by night
they saw a bright new shining star
And heard a choir from heaven sing
the music came from afar (to chorus)

VERSE 3) Now Joseph and his wife, Mary
came to Bethlehem that night
They found no place to bear her child
Not a single room was is sight (to verse 4)

VERSE 4) By and by they found a nook- in a stable all forlorn
and in a manger, cold and dark,
Mary's little child was born (to chorus)

Lift Up His Name

Words and Music by
BRYAN McCLAIN

If you want joy in your he- heart joy that will never depa-- ------rt Lift up His name

sing of His glory   Lift up His name   sing of His glory   lift up His name

sing of His glory and love-------

2) If you want love in your heart
3) If you want peace in your heart

Every Good and Perfect Gift

Words and Music by
JEREMY DALTON

Every good and perfect gift comes down from the Fa------ther

Every good and perfect gift comes down from the Fa----ther

Every good and perfect gift comes down from the Fa------ther

Every good and perfect gift comes down from the Fa----ther

118

Day By Day

STEPHEN SCHWARTZ

How Great Thou Art

STUART K. HINE

119

VERSE 2) When through the woods and forest glades I wander
And hear the birds sing sweetly in the trees
When I look down from lofty mountain grandeur
And hear the brook and feel the gentle breeze

VERSE 3) And when I think that God His son not sparing
Sent Him to die, I scarce can take it in
That on the cross, my burden gladly bearing
He bled and died to take away my sin

VERSE 4) When Christ shall come with shout of acclamation
And take me home, what joy shall fill my heart
Then I shall bow in humble adoration
And there proclaim, my God, how great Thou art

He's Everything to Me

Words and Music by
RALPH CARMICHAEL

Go Tell on the Mountain 121

Words: Paraphrase of Psalm 24 by JOHN YLVISAKER
Music: Traditional American

VERSE 2) The shepherds feared and trembled
when lo, above the earth
Rang out the angel chorus
that hailed our Savior's birth

VERSE 3) Down in a lowly manger
The humble Christ was born
And God sent us salvation
That blessed Christmas morn

Oh, How He Loves You and Me

KURT KAISER

We Are an Offering

Words and Music by
DWIGHT LILES

123

Thank You, My Lord

Words and Music by
HAL DAVID and ARCHIE P. JORDAN

1) Thank you my Lord for a beautiful day Thank you my Lord I'm so happy to say

Thank you my Lord for the flowers that grow There would be nothing I

know without You You

VERSE 2) Thank you, my Lord for the sun in the sky
Thank you, my Lord I'm so grateful that I
Thank you, my Lord for the rivers that flow

VERSE 3) Thank you, my Lord for the birds in the trees
Thank you, my Lord I am down on my knees
Thank you, my Lord for the rain and the snow

Clap Your Hands

Words and Music by
DWIGHT LILES

Clap your hands all you people

Shout to God for joy

He is king o----ver all---the earth His throne is established in

righteousness And now He comes His people to bless Clap your
Clap your hands

VERSE 2) God declares we are made overcomers
by Jesus' blood and the word of our faith
Now enter into the light of His presence
A joyful noise to our Father make

126

Holy, Holy

Words and Music by
JIMMY OWENS

2) Gracious father - we're so blessed to be your children
3) Precious Jesus - we're so glad that you've redeemed us
4) Holy Spirit - come and fill our lives anew
5) Hallelujah - and we lift our hearts before you

Let the People Praise

GRACE HAWTHORNE

127

BURYL RED

VERSE 2) Alleluia- Amen Let the people praise our God
Alleluia- Amen Let the people praise our God

Pass It On

Words and Music by
KURT KAISER

VERSE 2) What a wondrous time is spring when all the leaves
are budding
The birds begin to sing- the flowers start
their blooming
That's how it is with God's love- once you've
experienced it
you want to sing- it's fresh like spring;
You want to pass it on

VERSE 3) I wish for you my friend this happiness that
I've found
You can depend on Him- it matters not where
you're bound
I'll shout it from the mountain top
I want my world to know
The Lord of love has come to me- I want to pass it on

Morning Has Broken

Words: ELEANOR FARJEON
Music: Traditional Gaelic

VERSE2) Sweet the rains newfall-sunlit from heaven
Like the first dewfall- on the first grass
Praise for the sweetness - of the wet garden
Spring in completeness- where his feet pass

VERSE3) Mine is the sunlight-mine is the morning
Born of the one light- Eden saw play
Praise with elation- praise every morning
God's recreation- of the new day

In Christ, a New Creation

Words and Music by
JOHN YLVISAKER

130

VERSE 2) In Christ, a new creation-In Christ we are made new
The reconciliation- at last is coming true
In Christ, a new creation- ambassadors are we
Go out to every nation- and set the captive free

VERSE 3) In Christ, a new creation- In Christ we are made new
We feel the liberation- we feel God's presence too
In Christ, a new creation-reborn to live again
We sing for our salvation- We sing the great AMEN!

A Mighty Fortress

MARTIN LUTHER
Arr., Traditional

131

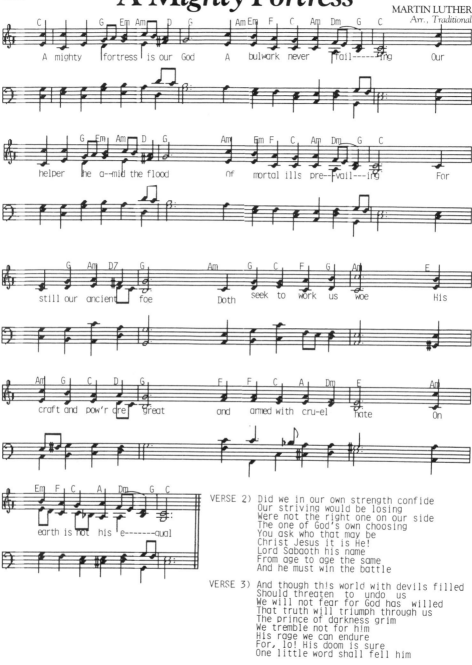

A mighty fortress is our God A bulwark never fail----ing Our

helper he a--mid the flood Of mortal ills pre--vail---ing For

still our ancient foe Doth seek to work us woe His

craft and pow'r are great and armed with cru-el hate On

earth is not his e-------qual

VERSE 2) Did we in our own strength confide
Our striving would be losing
Were not the right one on our side
The one of God's own choosing
You ask who that may be
Christ Jesus it is He!
Lord Sabaoth his name
From age to age the same
And he must win the battle

VERSE 3) And though this world with devils filled
Should threaten to undo us
We will not fear for God has willed
That truth will triumph through us
The prince of darkness grim
We tremble not for him
His rage we can endure
For, lo! His doom is sure
One little word shall fell him

VERSE 4) That word above all earthly powers
No thanks to them abideth
The spirit and the gifts are ours
Through God who with us sideth
Let goods and kindred go
This mortal life also
The body they may kill
God's truth abideth still
God's kingdom is forever

Such an Out of the Ordinary Man

JOHN WORRE
Arr. Henry Wiens

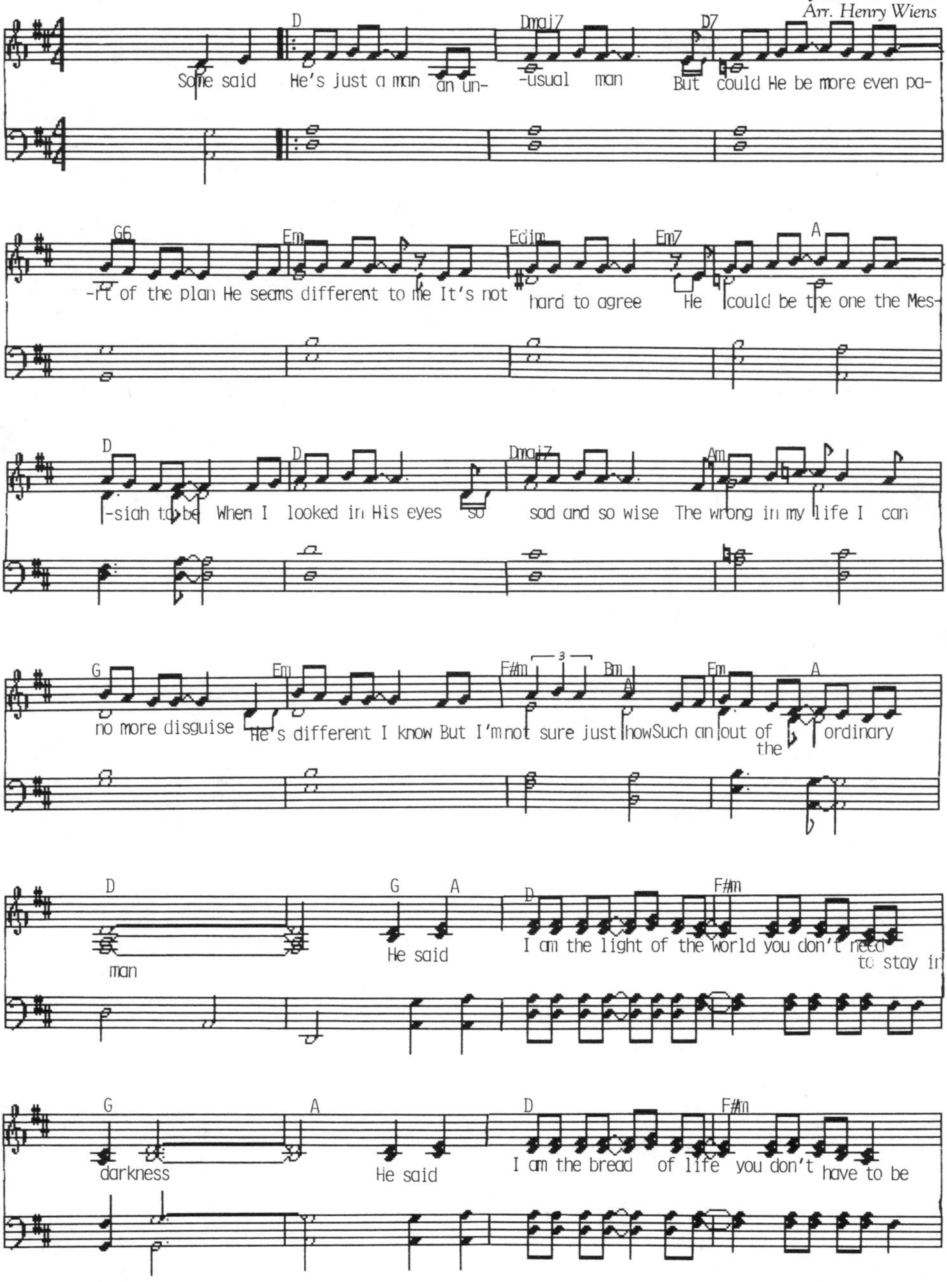
D Dmaj7 D7
Some said He's just a man an un- -usual man But could He be more even pa-
G6 Em Edim Em7 A
-rt of the plan He seems different to me It's not hard to agree He could be the one the Mes-
D D Dmaj7 Am
-siah to be When I looked in His eyes so sad and so wise The wrong in my life I can
G Em F#m 3 Bm Em A
no more disguise He's different I know But I'm not sure just how Such an out of the ordinary
D G A D F#m
man He said I am the light of the world you don't need to stay in
G A D F#m
darkness He said I am the bread of life you don't have to be

VERSE 2) He came humbly to John, tho' He was God's own Son,
To be an example to all of His own,
Said a voice from above-"This is my Son whom I love"
And God's Holy Spirit came down like a dove
He was baptized that day-in the water that way
But something more happened that made people say
So much power He has, So much wisdom He shows
Such an out of the ordinary man

VERSE 3) He taught how to live-that you get what you give
To the lost He had come for to seek and to save
He made blind eyes to see, set the captive ones free
Little children He said "Let them come unto me"
Such love He would show, and wherever He'd go
From Him living rivers of water would flow
He gave all He had- and He did what He said
Such an out of the ordinary man

Great Is the Lord

DEBORAH D. SMITH

MICHAEL W. SMITH
Arr. by Gary Rhodes

How Majestic Is Your Name   134

MICHAEL W. SMITH

O Lord our Lord how ma-jestic is your name in all the earth O Lord our Lord how ma--jes---tic is your name in all the earth O Lord we praise your name we magnify your name Prince of Peace Mighty God O Lord God Al-might----y

CONFESSION AND FORGIVENESS

Leader: Let us be honest with ourselves, our God, and with each other and confess our sins in order that we might receive the forgiveness of God and experience the joy of the community of Christ.

People: Lord, our God, we have sinned by what we have thought, said and done. We continue to pull away from You even though You love us with an everlasting love. Today in worship, we recognize our failures and our weaknesses. We confess our sins of omission and commission. We confess that we have not loved our neighbor as ourselves. We come to You now, as brothers and sisters in Christ, who need Your power and forgiveness.

Leader: In the name of Jesus, the Christ, I speak His word to you: "I belong to you as you belong to me. I am one of you, I know you. I died and rose for you so that your sin might be forgiven. I feel what you feel and I live through your life. I forgive your wrongs and with that forgiveness give you power to change your condition as you live lives that are pleasing in my sight."

AFFIRMATION OF FAITH

I believe in a living God, creator of all humankind, who has created and recreates the entire universe by power and love.

I believe in Jesus Christ, God in the flesh and my Savior and Lord. Because of His work, His death, His life and His suffering, I know who I am, what I can become through Christ.

I believe that God is present with us always and can be experienced in prayer, the Sacraments, the Word, the fellowhsip of believers and in all that we do.   Amen.

OPENING SENTENCES

Leader: Dear friends, let us love one another, for love comes from God.

People: We love because God first loved us.

Leader: If someone says, "I love God," yet hates their brother or sister, that person is a liar.

People: For one cannot love God, who is not seen, if one does not love a brother or sister, who is seen.

Leader: This, then, is the command that Christ gave us; anyone who loves God must also love their brother and sister.

People: O, Divine Master, grant that we may not so much seek to be consoled as to console; to be understood as to understand; to be loved as to love.   Amen.

CONFESSION (*reading together*)

Eternal God, we pray that You will listen as we confess our failures in love and friendship. We have talked about such things as caring, community and concern, but instead have shown anger, hostility and greed. We have talked about love, faith and hope, but have shown injustice, distrust, and apathy. We have talked about kindness, forgiveness and gentleness, but yet have shown hate, spite, and selfishness. Forgive the sins of our fallen condition; the sins of our broken promises; the sins that we dare not name. In the name of Jesus who was crucified for sin, forgive us.

DECLARATION OF PARDON

This is how God showed love for us; Jesus came into the world that we might have life. This is what love is. It is not that we have loved God, but that God loved us and sent Jesus to be the means by which our sins are forgiven.

AFFIRMATION OF FAITH

We confess that Jesus is the Christ, the Son of the Living God and that He takes away the sin of the world. By His name and grace we live our lives of mission and witness for the world. We confess that God is the creator of all people on earth and has created us to live in a covenant of love established through the Word and sacraments. Through Baptism we begin this new life that is acted out through the community of believers throughout the world. We rejoice with those who rejoice and we stand together with those who are sad. In the body and blood of Jesus we find the presence of Christ and forgiveness for our sin. Within the church of God we accept our place as missionary, prophet, teacher, helper and friend, in order that we might serve with great purpose the church that presently exists and the church that is to come. Praise, blessing, honor and glory be to God the Creator, Son and Holy Spirit, forever and ever.   Amen.

CONFESSION

Lord, God, today we pause again to confess our shortcomings in life and love. We want to live life to the fullest, but we always seem to become disillusioned or disappointed. We want to have deep, meaningful relationships, but we seem to short circuit those we love with our own selfishness. Lord, we need the power to change, but we realize now that we cannot do it on our own. We are sinful; we fall shrot of the mark; and we ask for Your forgiveness.

WE HEAR THE GOOD NEWS

The God of all creation has entered our human existence in the person of Jesus Christ. Through Him our sinful condition has been given new possibilities of faith and life. By His death and resurrection the price of our sin has been paid in full and we stand before God as new people. The Holy Spirit is present with us and in us to give us the power to live out this new life. By the spirit we have life. Praise God.

THE STATEMENT OF FAITH

We believe in God, creator of infinite wisdom, power, whose love points the direction of the universe and whose concern is for all of us.

We believe in Jesus Christ, the Son of God and the Savior of the world. Jesus is the true gift of the Creator's love, the reason for our hope, and the promise of forgiveness of sin and eternal life. We trust Him.

We believe in the Holy Spirit, God present with us, keeping us aligned to the truth of scripture and the example of Jesus, our Lord.

We believe that our relationship to God is born out of grace and acted out through deeds of love and mercy through the church of Christ. We can experience the true love of God in prayer, the Sacraments, the Word, and the fellowship of all believers. We desire that the kingdom of God would come to all people and the joy of Christ would be ours forever.   Amen.

CONFESSION

Lord, we confess our lack of life. We have traded abundant living for a cheap imitation. We have taken every shortcut possible on our way to where we're going. We have stepped on others in the process and have tripped over ourselves trying to find happiness in life. Lord, we need a resurrection. We need to be pulled from this life into a new existence where love powers our actions and peace lives in our heart.

ABSOLUTION

Our Lord knows our every need and gives new life to those who believe. The resurrection of Jesus Christ is our new beginning as the old things die and we are made new. Death no longer rules us and we look forward to eternal life with our Creator God. Our sin has been forgiven in the forever action of Jesus as He went to the cross and rose from the grave. We will live forever. Alleluia!

STATEMENT OF FAITH

We believe in God, who created all that exists and continues to recreate the lives of those who trust. We believe in Jesus Christ, the only Son of a loving God; whose purpose was to save a lost world and who now works in us and others by the Holy Spirit.

We believe that God is calling each of us to be a part of the body of Christ, to celebrate God's presence, to love and serve others, to stand against the powers of injustice and prejudice, and to declare for all the world to hear, "Jesus is risen and we are His people." Thanks be to God.

CONFESSION

Lord, we have been given life but we have not lived. We have enjoyed the wonder of Your creation, but have failed to acknowledge You as Creator. We have sought the full pleasure that life has to offer, but we feel like we have been shortchanged. Lord, we confess that we have separated ourselves from You by our thoughts, words and actions. We desire life to be what it was meant to be. We are in need of a Savior. Lord, forgive our sin and give us real life in You.

ABSOLUTION

Our God is the God of life. Our Creator God, who brought the worlds into being, created each of us, and desires only the best for us. God knows of our sin and has provided for our deliverance through Jesus, God with us. Jesus gave up His life so that we might live. Jesus' death was for our sin and for our daily relationship with Him. Our God is the God of life. As we trust God our life is made new and we can live together with God for now and throughout eternity. Praise God for the Gift of Life.

AFFIRMATION OF FAITH

I have faith in God, in response to overwhelming love.

I believe that God created me and all that I have and has given to me gifts beyond measure.

I have faith in Jesus, who emptied Himself out of His love for me.

I believe that Christ died on a cross for my sin, conquered death and the power of evil, and was raised to life on the third day. His death is mine, His resurrection is mine, new life is mine because of Jesus' words and work.

I believe in the Holy Sp;irit in response to overwhelming love.

I believe that the Holy Spirit is present here among us and lives within in each person. The Spirit continues to call people by the Gospel and creates and builds the church of Christ. Through the power of the Spirit I have power to stand in strength against all adversity.

I believe that Jesus is gone to prepare a place for me and will come again to take each of us to be with Him.   Amen.

CONFESSION

Lord, we need Your mercy. In this hour, help us to see our sin and pain and pray for a fresh start. Help us to see the shortcomings in our lives and look to You for the answers to our problems. Give us a new vision of what life can be like. Teach us to hope, to love, to give and to have faith. Lord, we need Your mercy.

ABSOLUTION — The Good News

Our God has heard the cries and felt your pain and has had mercy on us. God has seen our need and provided for our salvation; seen our condition and provided the solution; seen our heart and given us a Savior. Through the death and resurrection of Jesus Christ, our sin is no longer the weight that holds us down. We are free to live in victory, free from the sin of our self deceit and free from Satan's power. Praise God for goodness.

AFFIRMATION OF FAITH

We believe in God, the Creator of all things, the source of all goodness and love.

We believe in Jesus Christ, the Son of God, true God yet true man. He was crucified, died and was buried for our sin that we might be free and know the joy of life. He was raised on the third day and ascended to heaven, and will come again in power and glory to judge both the living and the dead.

We believe in the Holy Spirit, the power of God at work inside of us.

We believe in the church of God, the people of faith throughout the world.

We believe that our sin is forgiven and that we will live together with God for now and throughout eternity.   Amen.

CONFESSION

Lord, we confess our lack of faith. We see a glimpse of what we ought to be and we know we fall short of the goal. We desire faith that is solid and unchanging, yet we crumble under trials and temptations. We want to be strong, but we know our own weakness. Our sinful condition strips us of any spiritual gain that we humanly devise. Lord, forgive us. Accept us as we are, unworthy for the task, yet gifted for Your purposes. Give us Your gift of faith.

ABSOLUTION

Our God is a great God and knows our needs for all areas of our life. God knows our weakness and our unbelieving hearts, yet loves us enough to die on a cross and provide forgiveness of our sin. Now the focus is not on the faith that we can muster, but on the great gifts that our Lord gives daily as we live in trust. God has given us the gift of faith, faith for the moment, faith for every trial, faith for every temptation, faith for every difficult situation. Praise God for this inexpressible gift of faith.

AFFIRMATION OF FAITH

I have faith in God, in response to overwhelming love.

I believe that God created me and all that I have, and has given to me gifts beyond measure.

I have faith in Jesus, who emptied Himself out of His love for me.

I believe that Christ died on a cross for my sin, conquered death and the power of evil, and was raised to life on the third day. His death is mine, His resurrection is mine, new life is mine because of Jesus' words and work.

I believe in the Holy Spirit in response to overwhelming love.

I believe that the Holy Spirit is present here among us and lives within in each person. The Spirit continues to call people by the Gospel, and creates and builds the church of Christ. Through the power of the Spirit I have power to stand in strength against all adversity.

I believe that Jesus is preparing a place for me and will come again to take each of us to be with Him.   Amen.

CONFESSION

Lord, we confess that we have heard the call but have chosen not to follow. We have picked roads that lead to anxiety and despair. We have walked paths of darkenss and sorrow. We have run from Your beckoning love. Lord, we come in worship today asking for a new beginning. We want to be cleansed and made right. We desire direction and purpose for our living. We need our sins forgiven.

ABSOLUTION

God's eternal love for us calls us to a new life today. God has provided the complete plan for our life. Jesus' death on the cross has paid the price for our sinful condition, breaking us free to be true believers. Jesus calls us to take up His cross and follow Him. Through the Holy Spirit we are given the power to respond to that call; the power to change direction; the power to make new and different choices; and the power to live life as it was meant to be. Today we can truly celebrate following Jesus.

AFFIRMATION OF FAITH

I believe in God, the Creator of all life, the source of all love, and the giver of every good and perfect gift.

I believe in Jesus, God's only Son, who was born of a virgin, who lived as no other man has lived, and who suffered and died for the sin of all the world. I believe that Jesus' death and resurrection has given me new life and I will live with Him for all eternity.

I believe in the Holy Spirit — God with us. I have been called by the Spirit, enlightened by the Spirit, and gifted for service by the Spirit. God is at work today and the Holy Spirit is the vessel for God's continued love and concern for us. I believe that I can know and experience God in prayer, forgiveness, the sacraments, the fellowship of the church and all that we do.

We confess the distance that we have made between us. We confess that we have taken the beauty of creation and used it for our own glory. We confess that we have not taken Your death and resurrection seriously. We have played church games and skirted the real issues. We confess that each day of our life is filled with inner pressure that we feel powerless to control. Oh God, who knows us as we are, restore within us a new sense of Your daily activity. Shatter our apathy with Your creative wonders, Your redemptive action, and Your Spirit's power.

WE HEAR THE GOOD NEWS

God has provided for our every need. God has provided a world of untold wonder in the beauty of the landscape and the complexity of each of us. God has given us the freedom to choose and we by nature tend to choose our own ways instead of God's ways. This nature separates us from our Creator; so God provided the perfect way to communicate with us, by sending Jesus. Our sinful nature was put to death with Jesus on the Cross and we rise to new life with Jesus in His resurrection. Today the Holy Spirit lives in us and God is active in every day to change our attitudes, direct our thoughts, and rearrange our desires. Praise God for everlasting love.

STATEMENT OF FAITH

I believe in God, the almighty, creator of heaven and earth.

I believe in Jesus Christ, God's only Son, our Lord. He was conceived by the power of the Holy Spirit and born of the virgin Mary. He suffered under Pontius Pilate, was crucified, died, and was buried. He descended into hell. On the third day He rose again. He ascended into heaven, and is seated at God's right hand. He will come again to judge the living and the dead.

I believe in the Holy Spirit, the holy catholic Church, the communion of saints, the forgiveness of sins, the resurrection of the body, and the life everlasting.   Amen.

CONFESSION

Gracious God, who is the source of all love, we have been called to share not only our lives but our livelihood and have found it difficult. We have been called to respond in total love to the needs that surround us but have found that kind of commitment unattractive. The need is great and our hearts are hard. Help us today to discover the great joy of sharing the adventure of giving and the wonder of Your spirit at work in us. We desire a new beginning. Forgive our sin and give us a new start.

ABSOLUTION

Hear the word of the Gospel! The God of all the universe has loved you with an everlasting love that forgets our sin and makes all things new. Hear the word of the Gospel! Jesus Christ, the Son of God, died on the cross so that our relationship with God would be made right. Hear the word of the Gospel! "For the love of Christ controls us, because we are convinced that one has died for all. I have been crucified with Christ; it is no longer I who live but Christ who lives in me; and the life I now live in the flesh I live by faith in the Son of God, who loved me and gave Himself for me." Praise God for the good news of the Gospel!

AFFIRMATION OF FAITH

I believe in God, my Creator.

I believe in Jesus, God's Son, my Lord, who suffered died and was buried. He descended into hell and on the third day rose again and sits at God's right hand. Jesus will come again to judge all people.

I believe in the Holy Spirit, God with me. I believe God will triumph in the final battle when righteousness will reign and God will rule. I believe that I will be raised to new life in my Lord and I will live for eternity.   Amen.

CONFESSION

Lord, we have heard Your call to "go" and "tell the world," but we have not responded. Forgive our lack of courage and commitment. We have heard You saying to us, "Be full of love for others, following the example of Christ who loved you," but we even find it difficult to love ourselves. Today we confess that we are not worthy of Your love and ask that You would forgive the sin of every area of our life. We desire a new sensitivity to the larger world around us. Open our hearts that we may hear their voices. Open our eyes that we may see their agony. Open our minds that we may understand their needs. Open our hearts that we may become involved.

ABSOLUTION

Our God is a great God and has forgiven our sin to set us free. Out of God's great love for us, Jesus died on the cross and rose on the third day so that the gap between us and God chould be closed. Out of great love for us, God provides for our every need in our daily life. Out of great love for us, God gives us the power to respond to the needs of those around us by giving us a new desire. Out of great love for us, our sin is forgiven, we are free, thanks be to God.

AFFIRMATION OF FAITH

I believe in God, the almighty, creator of heaven and earth.

I believe in Jesus Christ, God's only Son, our Lord. He was conceived by the power of the Holy Spirit and born of the virgin Mary. He suffered under Pontius Pilate, was crucified, died, and was buried. He descended into hell. On the third day He rose again. He ascended into heaven, and is seated at God's right hand. He will come again to judge the living and the dead.

I believe in the Holy Spirit, the holy catholic Church, the communion of saints, the forgiveness of sins, the resurrection of the body, and the life everlasting.   Amen.

CONFESSION

Lord, we have been called to follow You but we have not responded. We have been commanded to love one another, but we continue in our old ways. We have been told to spread the Good News of Your love to every part of our world, but have found the mission too difficult. We have not loved You with our whole heart and our neighbors as ourselves. We come today looking for Good News. Forgive our sin.

ABSOLUTION

Today there is Good News! God has forgiven our sin so that we might love each other the way we were inteded to love. In our failures and in our desperation God picks us up and breathes new power into our needy lives. The eternal love of God is made ours in the death of Jesus on the cross, to pay for our sin and separation. God's love is the Good News for everyone today.

THE APOSTLES' CREED

I believe in God, the almighty, creator of heaven and earth.

I believe in Jesus Christ, God's only Son, our Lord. He was conceived by the power of the Holy Spirit and born of the virgin Mary. He suffered under Pontius Pilate, was crucified, died, and was buried. He dcescended into hell. On the third day He rose again. He ascended into heaven, and is seated at God's right hand. He will come again to judge the living and the dead.

I believe in the Holy Spirit, the holy catholic Church, the communion of saints, the forgiveness of sins, the resurrection of the body, and the life everlasting.   Amen.

CONFESSION

Lord, we are a restless people. As the weight of the world increases we look everywhere for release. We confess today that we have not found solutions to our problems or deliverance from our burdens. We desire peace. Our hearts need a resting place where the worries of everyday life are in perspective and where the sin of our life is forgiven. Lord, give us peace and forgive our sin.

ABSOLUTION

Our God is a God of peace. God says, "Come to me, all who are tired from carrying heavy loads and I will give you rest. Take my yoke and put it on you, and learn from me, because I am gentle and humble in spirit; and you will find rest." The peace we desperately seek is ours through Christ Jesus. The weight of our sin has been taken by Him in His death and resurrection. We no longer are carrying our sin but we are free; released from sin's burden. We can be at peace because of God's great love for us as children. Praise God for love and peace.

AFFIRMATION OF FAITH

I believe in God, the almighty, creator of heaven and earth.

I believe in Jesus Christ, God's only Son, our Lord. He was conceived by the power of the Holy Spirit and born of the virgin Mary. He suffered under Pontius Pilate, was crucified, died, and was buried. He descended into hell. On the third day He rose again. He ascended into heaven, and is seated at God's right hand. He will come again to judge the living and the dead.

I believe in the Holy Spirit, the holy catholic Church, the communion of saints, the forgiveness of sins, the resurrection of the body, and the life everlasting.   Amen.

CONFESSION

Lord, I feel blind. My life seems like a long, dark hallway with no end in sight. I struggle from one step to another, trying not to fall, but sometimes I can't help myself. Lord, swing wide the doors! Open the windows! Let in the new light of Your love. Light the paths that I walk so that I can understand where I have been and so that I can be confident of the direction I am headed. Give me Your gift of faith so that my life is no longer weighted down with sin, but freed up to live life and serve others.

ABSOLUTION

Our God is a great God! God has provided for our every need. Through the death and resurrection of Jesus Christ, we are given the infinite possibilities of abundant life on earth and eternal life with God. The darkness of our sin has been changed by the light of the love of Jesus. God's gift of faith is the beginning of a new direction as every darkened corner of our life is filled with light and every unspeakable sin is forgiven. We are free to walk by faith in the light of God's unending love.

AFFIRMATION OF FAITH

God is love, and in God is the source of all goodness and turth. God is the creator of the universe and continues to recreate with us a kingdom of compassion for all humankind.

Jesus is God's Son. Jesus was born of Mary, lived a life of kindness and concern, died a cruel death on an executioner's cross, and was raised on the third day to new life. Jesus' life is my life. I can now live a life of kindness and concern I can die and be raised to new life; I can live as a forgiven sinner, confident of my place in eternity.

The Holy Spirit is the spirit of God, alive and at work, establishing and building the Kingdom of God on this earth. The Spirit of God leads me into the true faith, guides me through the difficult choices of life, and comforts me when I feel as if I cannot go on. God is with me, living inside of me, through the Holy Spirit.

CONFESSION

Lord, we come to You today in need of forgiveness. We have believed the words of the false prophets who have led us into selfish materialism and empty humanism. Forgive the sins of our fallen condition. We have believed the words of those who have told us that we can change ourselves with manufactured love. Forgive the sin of our fallen condition. We have believed the words of those who promised salvation through false gods. Forgive the sins of our fallen condition.

WE HEAR ABOUT FORGIVENESS

Today our God comes to us with a new word proclaiming forgiveness for all sinners. This word shouts freedom for the captives and new life for those who were dead. This word brings hope for the defenseless and eternal life for those who trust in the Lord. This word comes to life for each of us in the person of Jesus Christ, whose death for our sin assures us of our forgiveness. Praise God for this life-giving Word.

AFFIRMATION OF FAITH

I believe in God, my Creator.

I believe in Jesus, God's Son, my Lord, who suffered, died and was buried. He descended into hell and on the third day rose again and sits at God's right hand. Jesus will come again to judge all people.

I believe in the Holy Spirit, God with me. I believe God will triumph in the final battle when righteousness will reign and God will rule. I believe that I will be raised to new life in my Lord and I will live for eternity.   Amen.

CONFESSION

Lord, we have heard Your words of love, but they continue to fall on deaf ears. Your Word of forgiveness is clearly for us but instead we choose to listen to other lords. We have turned away in our desperate search for our own fulfillment. We have betrayed ourselves by what we think, say and do. We are empty, Lord. Fill us with Your Word of love.

ABSOLUTION

God's Word is clear today. If we confess our sin, God is faithful, and will forgive our sin and cleanse us from the impurities of our life. God's Word is clear today. Our old self was crucified with Jesus so that the sinful body might be destroyed and we might no longer be enslaved to sin. God's Word is clear today. While we were helpless, Christ died for the ungodly. God loved the world and gave a Son, that whoever believes in Him should not perish but have eternal life. God's Word is our Word of love.

AFFIRMATION OF FAITH

We believe in one God, the Father, the Almighty, maker of heaven and earth, of all that is, seen and unseen.

We believe in one Lord, Jesus Christ, the only Son of God, eternally begotten of the Father, God from God, Light from Light, true God from true God, begotten, not made, of one Being with the Father. Through Him all things were made. For us and for our salvation He came down from heaven; by the power of the Holy Spirit He became incarnate from the virgin Mary, and was made man. For our sake He was crucified under Pontius Pilate; He suffered death and was buried. On the third day He rose again in accordance with the Scriptures; He ascended into heaven and is seated at the right hand of the Father. He will come again in glory to judge the living and the dead, and His kingdom will have no end.

We believe in the Holy Spirit, the Lord, the giver of life, who proceeds from the Father and the Son. With the Father and the Son He is worshiped and glorified. He has spoken through the prophets. We believe in one holy catholic and apostolic Church. We acknowledge one Baptism for the forgiveness of sins. We look for the resurrection of the dead, and the life of the world to come.   Amen.

CONFESSION

Lord, we confess our lack of faith. You have promised to provide for all of our needs, and yet we mistrust Your promise. We know the futility of our own ambitions and our inability to do that which we desire. Today we recognize the sin within us, and ask that You would forgive us. Lord, in Your mercy, give us daily bread, not only for our bodies but as food for our spirits. Forgive our sin and cleanse us so that we can be people pleasing in Your sight and ministers in Your service.

ABSOLUTION

Our God is a great God and provides for all of our needs. God gives us daily bread and supplies for every spiritual need. Our sin no longer controls us. Our response to this love is the focus for our lives. The death of Jesus Christ has paid the cost of our sin and has freed us to live in victory. We are forgiven. We are sons and daughters of the King. We are ministers to each other. Praise God for the daily provision of our every need.

AFFIRMATION OF FAITH

I believe in a great God who created the world in power and love and whose character is reflected in all of creation.

I believe in Jesus Christ, Son of God and Son of Man. His life, His teachings, His miracles, His death and His resurrection combine to provide true forgiveness of sin and life for all eternity. His strength bolsters my weakness, His love covers my failures and His sacrifice forgives my sin. I trust Him as a friend and brother, a Savior and Lord.

I believe in the Holy Spirit, God at work in and among us. I believe that God is present and active in today's world and that I can know some of the joy of heaven right now. I believe that the church of Christ is the people of God and that in prayer, the sacraments, and the fellowship of the church we can experience true meaning and everlasting love in our lives.

CONFESSION

Lord, we confess our lack of power. We sometimes feel helpless, alone, and weak. We realize now that each time we try to do everything on our own, we fail. Lord, we need Your power. We need to rely on You daily to do the things that are necessary for our life. We want Your power to be ours so that we can stand tall in Your world. We need to be reassured that death need not be feared and that true life is found in You.

ABSOLUTION

The God that we worship here today is a great God! In creation we see a glimpse of God's power and majesty. In God's Son we see ultimate love for us in action. In the Holy Spirit we see ongoing encouragement and power for every day. Our God is a great God! Jesus has forgiven our sin and made a right relationship between us. God has given us all the gifts necessary to do the work of a believer. Praise God for love and kindness.

AFFIRMATION OF FAITH

I have faith in God, in response to overwhelming love.

I believe that God created me and all that I have, and has given to me gifts beyond measure.

I have faith in Jesus, who emptied himself out of His love for me.

I believe that Christ died on a cross for my sin, conquered death and the power of evil, and was raised to life on the third day. His death is mine, His resurrection is mine, new life is mine because of Jesus' words and work.

I believe in the Holy Spirit in response to overwhelming love.

I believe that the Holy Spirit is present here among us and lives within each person. The Spirit continues to call people by the Gospel, and creates and builds the church of Christ. Through the power of the Spirit I have power to stand in strength against all adversity.

I believe that Jesus is preparing a place for me and will come again to take each of us to be with Him.   Amen.

CONFESSION

God, our Creator, we confess our shortcomings in life and love. We confess that we do not desire Your love and sometimes we even turn our back on Your love. Lord, we need to hear again that You care for us! We want to become more like You in every way. Forgive this distance we have placed between us and restore our relationship of love.

ABSOLUTION

Our God loves with an unconditional love that accepts us as we are. God has forgiven our sin by giving Jesus to die for us. Love is perfect! God loves us even when we turn our backs and run away. God comes to us today offering true life and real love to those who believe. Praise God for Grace!

AFFIRMATION OF FAITH

I believe in God, my Creator.

I believe in Jesus, God's Son, my Lord, who suffered, died and was buried. He descended into hell and on the third day rose again and sits at God's right hand. Jesus will come again to judge all people.

I believe in the Holy Spirit, God with me. I believe God will triumph in the final battle when righteousness will reign and God will rule. I believe that I will be raised to new life in my Lord and I will live for eternity.   Amen.

CONFESSION

Lord, we confess that we have not been listening. We have been deaf to Your call in many ways. We have heard the words and the songs, yet have gone our own way. Today Lord, we confess our sin and want to be made right with You, so that we can be made right with our brothers and sisters. Give us ears to hear You and open hearts to accept Your loving grace.

ABSOLUTION

Our God is persistent, continues to call us, even when we turn our back. God continues to love us even when we do not return love. Ultimate love for us was shown as God sent Jesus to the cross to die in our place for our sin. Today God calls each of us to lay down our weight of sin and come home.

AFFIRMATION OF FAITH

I believe in a living God, creator of all humankind, who has created and recreates the entire universe by power and love.

I believe in Jesus Christ, God in the flesh, and my Savior and Lord. Because of His work, His death, His life, and His suffering, I know who I am, what I can become through Christ.

I believe that God is present with us always and can be experienced in prayer, the Sacraments, the Word, the fellowship of believers and in all that we do.   Amen.

CONFESSION

Lord, we desire life. We have traded our lives for a cheap imitation which leaves us unfulfilled and wanting. We have rejected the life that You offer in favor of our own manufactured pleasures. We have sold out to the vendors of this world and wonder why our life is empty. Lord, forgive the sin of our lifelessness and bring us to Yourself again.

ABSOLUTION

Our God is life, the creator of all life, the sustainer of all life, and the giver of life eternal. Real life is found in trusting God for all things. God gave the life of Jesus, who took our place on the cross of death in order that we might live. Jesus conquered death and offers that power to each of us who trust Him. Praise God for the possibility of new life.

AFFIRMATION OF FAITH

I believe in God, my Creator.

I believe in Jesus, God's Son, my Lord, who suffered, died and was buried. He descended into hell and on the third day rose again and sits at God's right hand. Jesus will come again to judge all people.

I believe in the Holy Spirit, God with me. I believe God will triumph in the final battle when righteousness will reign and God will rule. I believe that I will be raised to new life in my Lord and I will live for eternity.   Amen.

CONFESSION

Lord, we confess our sin in life and love. We turned away at every opportunity and treated You as a crisis God. Lord, forgive our sin, make us right, restore our relationship. We have been slow to forgive others. Allow us the freedom to live in relationship with our brothers and sisters.

ABSOLUTION

Our God says for now and for all time — "You are forgiven! I have set you free!" The sin that has weighed so heavily upon us has been lifted by God who gives forgiveness. This forgiveness is ours because of the death and resurrection of Jesus Christ, and from now on we can live as new creatures in a new creation. Jesus has given His forgiveness gift so that we might live forever. This gift allows us to step out in faith and forgive our brothers and sisters and live in harmony. Praise God for forgiveness.

THE STATEMENT OF FAITH

We believe in God, creator of infinite wisdom and power, whose love points the direction of the universe and whose concern is for all of us.

We believe in Jesus Christ, the Son of God and the Savior of the world. Jesus is the true gift of the Creator's love, the reason for our hope, and the promise of forgiveness of sin and eternal life. We trust Him.

We believe in the Holy Spirit, God present with us, keeping us aligned to the truth of scripture and the example of Jesus, our Lord.

We believe that our relationship to God is born out of grace and acted out through deeds of love and mercy through the chruch of Christ. We can experience the true love of God in prayer, the Sacraments, the Word, and the fellowship of all believers. We desire that the kingdom of God would come to all people and the joy of Christ would be ours forever.   Amen.

CONFESSION

Lord, we have heard Your call to discipleship but have listened to other Lords. We have felt the pull of Your Spirit, but have turned to other pursuits. We have seen our own lack of meaning, yet have looked in places that are empty. Lord, forgive our sin and cleanse us from the thoughts that destroy us and the actions that betray us.

ABSOLUTION

Our God is a great God and knows our every need. God has forgiven our sin and cleansed us from the thoughts and actions which pull us apart. Jesus, in His death on the cross, has paid the eternal price for our daily relationship with God. Through the Holy Spirit we are called, and enlightened so that we can truly be disciples living in the power and victory of the grace of God.

THE APOSTLES' CREED

I believe in God, the almighty, creator of heaven and earth.

I believe in Jesus Christ, God's only Son, our Lord. He was conceived by the power of the Holy Spirit and born of the virgin Mary. He suffered under Pontius Pilate, was crucified, died, and was buried. He descended into hell. On the third day He rose again. He ascended into heaven, and is seated at God's right hand. He will come again to judge the living and the dead.

I believe in the Holy Spirit, the holy catholic Church, the communion of saints, the forgiveness of sins, the resurrection of the body, and the life everlasting.   Amen.

CONFESSION

Lord, we confess that we have talked about love and reached grand conclusions, but have not really loved as You intended. We have instead showed indifference, anger, and hostility. Lord, we need a savior. We need to be delivered from this sin that separates us from You and Yours. We need You to be real for us today.

ABSOLUTION

Our Lord is a Lord of love. God caused love to come into existence and demonstrated that ultimate love in giving Jesus to die for each one of us that our sin might be forgiven. Love has been given to each of us, freely, and forever. We need not change or become different to receive this love. God invites us to come as we are! Praise God for love that forgives and forgets.

AFFIRMATION

We confess that Jesus is the Christ, the Son of the Living God and that He takes away the sin of the world. By His name and grace we live our lives of mission and witness for the world. We confess that God is the Creator of all people on earth and has created us to live in a covenant of love established through the Word and Sacraments. Through Baptism we begin this new life that is acted out through the community of believers throughout the world. We rejoice with those who rejoice and we stand together with those who are sad. In the body and blood of Jesus we find the presence of Christ and forgiveness for our sin. Within the church of God we accept our place as missionary, prophet, teacher, helper and friend in order that we might serve with great purpose the church that presently exists and the church that is to come. Praise, blessing, honor and glory be to God the Creator, Son and Holy Spirit, forever and ever.   Amen.

CONFESSION

Lord, have mercy on us. In this hour help us to see our sin and desire a fresh start with You. Help us see the shortcomings of our lives and look to You for the answers to our problems. Give us a new vision of what life can be like. Teach us to hope, to love, to give and to have faith. Lord, have mercy on us for we deserve only Your anger.

ABSOLUTION

Our God has heard the cries of lost people and has had mercy on us. God has seen our need and provided for our salvation; seen our condition and provided the solution; seen our heart and given us a Savior. Through the death and resurrection of Jesus Christ, our sin is no longer the weight that holds us down. We are free to live in victory, free from the sin of our self-deceit and free from Satan's power. Praise God for freedom.

AFFIRMATION OF FAITH

We believe in God, the Creator of all things, the source of all goodness and love.

We believe in Jesus Christ, the Son of God, true God, yet true man. He was crucified, died and was buried for our sin, that we might be free and know the joy and peace of life. He was raised on the third day and ascended to heaven, and will come again in power and glory to judge both the living and the dead.

We believe in the Holy Spirit, the power of God at work inside of us.

We believe in the church of God, the people of faith throughout the world.

We believe that our sin is forgiven and that we will live together with God for now and throughout eternity.   Amen.

CONFESSION

Lord, we confess our lack of faith. We see a glimpse of what we ought to be and we know we fall short of the goal. We desire faith that is unswerving and solid, yet we crumble under trials and temptations. We want to be strong, but we know our own weakness. Our sinful condition strips us of gains we humanly devise. Lord, forgive us. Accept us as we are, unworthy for the task yet gifted for Your purposes. Give us Your gift of faith.

ABSOLUTION

Our God is a great God and knows our needs for all areas of our life. God knows our weakness and our unbelieving hearts. God loves us enough to go to the cross to prove it, and in going to the cross provides for the forgiveness of our sin. Now the focus is not on the faith that we can muster, but on the great gifts that are ours daily as we trust. One of the gifts is faith...faith for the moment...faith for every trial...faith for every temptation. Praise God for the gift of faith.

AFFIRMATION OF FAITH

I believe in God, the almighty, creator of heaven and earth.

I believe in Jesus Christ, God's only Son, our Lord. He was conceived by the power of the Holy Spirit and born of the virgin Mary. He suffered under Pontius Pilate, was crucified, died, and was buried. He descended into hell. On the third day He rose again. He ascended into heaven, and is seated at God's right hand. He will come again to judge the living and the dead.

I believe in the Holy Spirit, the holy catholic Church, the communion of saints, the forgiveness of sins, the resurrection of the body, and the life everlasting.   Amen.

CONFESSION

O God, deliver us from this death of sin, from ourselves and our selfish ambition. Break the chains of guilt that gind us and hold us back. Deliver us from the illusion that we are self-sufficient. Open our eyes, bind our wounds and forgive this sin.

ABSOLUTION

God is a great God...the God of our deliverance. Just as God delivered the people of Israel out of Egypt, we will be delivered from our sin. Just as God brought the Israelites out of slavery, we will be delivered from our sin. To those who trust, God gives the power to become the people of God.

AFFIRMATION OF FAITH

I have faith in God, in response to overwhelming love.

I believe that God created me and all that I have, and has given to me gifts beyond measure.

I have faith in Jesus, who emptied himself out of His love for me.

I believe that Christ died on a cross for my sin, conquered death and the power of evil, and was raised to life on the third day. His death is mine, His resurrection is mine, new life is mine because of Jesus' words and work.

I believe in the Holy Spirit in response to overwhelming love.

I believe that the Holy Spirit is present here among us and lives within each person. The Spirit continues to call people by the Gospel, and creates and builds the church of Christ. Through the power of the Spirit I have power to stand in strength against all adversity.

I believe that Jesus is preparing a place for me and will come again to take each of us to be with Him.   Amen.

CONFESSION

We confess our lack of peace. We are unsettled and temporary. Our emotions drift from one point to another keeping us on edge. We try to structure our world for maximum protection, yet we find our fortress of self-sufficiency penetrated daily. Lord, we need to find your peace. We want to know that You love us and that our sin is forgiven. We want to stretch out and rest in Your loving arms. Lord forgive the distance we have placed between us.

ABSOLUTION

God is a great God! God has forgiven our sin. With love, God brings the gifts of peace, patience, and kindness. God's love is the motivation for our love and we can never be the same. God's peace becomes ours as we give more of ourselves. We can live confidently, knowing that our strength is in Christ, and that the pressure of our life has been relieved through God's kindness. Jesus' death and resurrection has set us free to know real peace.

AFFIRMATION OF FAITH

We believe in God, the Creator of all things, the source of all goodness and love.

We believe in Jesus Christ, the Son of God, true God, yet true man. He was crucified, died and was buried for our sin, that we might be free and know the joy and peace of life. He was raised on the third day and ascended to heaven, and will come again in power and glory to judge both the living and the dead.

We believe in the Holy Spirit, the power of God at work inside of us.

We believe in the church of God, the people of faith throughout the world.

We believe that our sin is forgiven and that we will live together with God for now and throughout eternity.   Amen.

CONFESSION

Lord, we confess that we sometimes behave like slaves rather than heirs to the throne. We have forgotten how much You love us and have placed a great distance between us in our relationship. Lord, we desire to start over — to be reunited — to begin again. We need Your love and we want to live in relationship with You. Forgive us — heal us — and make us inheritors of Your grace.

ABSOLUTION

Our God is a great God over all the universe, who rules by love and reigns with power. We are God's children. God loves us and showed this love by sending Jesus to the cross to die for our sin. All the riches of the kingdom belong to us because of Jesus. We now have a home, a place to live, and eternal life. Praise God.

STATEMENT OF FAITH

We believe in God, who created all that exists and continues to recreate the lives of those who trust. We believe in Jesus Christ, the only Son of a loving God; whose purpose was to save a lost world and who now works in us and others by the Holy Spirit.

We believe that God is calling each of us to be a part of the body of Christ, to celebrate God's presence, to love and serve others, to stand against the powers of injustice and prejudice, and to declare for all the world to hear, "Jesus is risen and we are His people." Thanks be to God.

PRAYER OF CONFESSION

We often seek the waters of life but we remain thirsty. We like the trinkets of the world even though they rust in our hands. We claim Your creation as our own and proceed to destroy the balance of Your order. We seek out love everywhere, yet forget Your love. Lord of Grace, lay bare the sadness of our human condition, and show us again our need for a Savior.

WE HEAR THE GOOD NEWS

God, our Creator, has given us the ultimate gift. God's gift to us is grace — everlasting love regardless of our attempts to reject it. God's gift is Christ's resurrection which is the open sign to all the world that love is real and that new life is for each of us. God's grace is sufficient for every need — including our salvation.

STATEMENT OF FAITH

We believe in God, who created all that exists and continues to recreate the lives of those who trust. We believe in Jesus Christ, the only Son of a loving God; whose purpose was to save a lost world and who now works in us and others by the Holy Spirit.

We believe that God is calling each of us to be a part of the body of Christ, to celebrate God's presence, to love and serve others, to stand against the powers of injustice and prejudice, and to declare for all the world to hear, "Jesus is risen and we are His people." Thanks be to God.

CONFESSION

Lord, we confess our lack of freedom. We are imprisoned by the sin which separates us from You. We are bound by our own humanity and desire a better existence. We are locked in our own prison of guilt, hopelessness and self-centerdness. We want to be free. We want to be able to celebrate life and all that You have to offer.

ABSOLUTION

God, our Creator, has freed us from our sin through the death and resurrection of Jesus Christ. God has unlocked the door, broken the chains, and set us free for a new life. All that we can be is ours as we trust God. Praise God for the freeing power of forgiveness.

STATEMENT OF FAITH

We believe in God, creator of infinite wisdom, power, whose love points the direction of the universe and whose concern is for all of us.

We believe in Jesus Christ, the Son of God and the Savior of the world. Jesus is the true gift of love, the reason for our hope, and the promise of forgiveness of sin and eternal life. We trust Him.

We believe in the Holy Spirit, God present with us, keeping us aligned to the truth of scripture and the example of Jesus, our Lord.

We believe that our relationship to God is born our of grace and acted out through deeds of love and mercy through the church of Christ. We can experience the true love of God in prayer, the sacraments, the Word, and the fellowship of all believers. We desire that the kingdom of God would come to all people and the joy of Christ would be ours forever.   Amen.

CONFESSION

God, our Creator, we confess our sin which weighs us down and burdens us daily. We come again to ask Your forgiveness for what we are and desire that You would make us what we can become. We confess our broken relationships, our weak discipleship and our poor image of ourselves. We come to You today, wounded and in need of Your new life. Lord, in Your mercy, hear our prayer.

ABSOLUTION

People of God — you are forgiven! This is the good news of salvation for those who trust. God has healed those broken relationships, given power for our discipleship, and given us a new picture of our own worth. The power of God is ours through the spirit that lives within. We no longer need to be burdered by our sin, but can stand tall and rejoice with other Christians for what God has done.

AFFIRMATION OF FAITH

We confess that Jesus is the Christ, the Son of the Living God and that He takes away the sin of the world. By His name and grace we live our lives of mission and witness for the world. We confess that God is the Creator of all people on earth and has created us to live in a covenant of love established through the Word and sacraments. Through Baptism we begin this new life that is acted out through the community of believers throughout the world. We rejoice with those who rejoice and we stand together with those who are sad. In the body and blood of Jesus we find the presence of Christ and forgiveness for our sin. Within the church of God we accept our place as missionary, prophet, teacher, helper and friend, in order that we might serve with great purpose the church that presently exists and the church that is to come. Praise, blessing, honor and glory be to God the Creator, Son and Holy Spirit, forever and ever.   Amen.

CONFESSION

Lord, we confess that we are powerless to do anything about our sad sitaution. We recognize that often the harder we try, the more we fail. We desire to be like others, but yet find fault with everything they do. Lord, fill us up with a new power that comes only from You. Allow us to realize that our sin has separated us from You, and that this sin robs us of the power that You desire to give to us. Lord, in this hour, send Your Holy Spirit and give us Your lifegiving power.

ABSOLUTION

God has provided for our every need. Through the ultimate sacrifice of Jesus, God has bridged the gap between us, and has dealt with our sin forever. We no longer need to be trapped by our sin but we have the power to overcome what we are and reach out to what God would have us be. The power of God is ours through the Holy Spirit which dwells within; motivating us to acts of kindness and mercy. Praise God for the gift of forgiveness.

AFFIRMATION OF FAITH

I believe in a living God, Creator of all humankind, who has created and recreates the entire universe by power and love.

I believe in Jesus Christ, God in the flesh and my Savior and Lord. Because of His work, His death, His life and His suffering, I know who I am, what I can become through Christ.

I believe that God is present with us always and can be experienced in prayer, the Sacraments, the Word, the fellowhsip of believers and in all that we do.   Amen.

CONFESSION

Lord, we confess our sin. You have showered us with blessings beyond compare, but we have chosen to turn our back to You. You have given us everything that we need to live a joyful life, yet we complain and desire more. You continue to give Your love to us daily, yet we choose to manufacture our own love. Lord of our failures and disappointments, we bow before You today asking for Your forgiveness.

ABSOLUTION

Our God created us to live in harmony. Although our sin separates us, God has provided the means by which our sins can be forgiven. The death and resurrection of Jesus Christ has reunited us with God. We who trust God with our life have the power to be what we were intended to be. Praise God for life-giving love.

AFFIRMATION OF FAITH

We believe in God, the Creator of all things, the source of all goodness and love.

We believe in Jesus Christ, the Son of God, true God yet true man. He was crucified, died and was buried for our sin that we might be free and know the joy of life. He was raised on the third day and ascended to heaven, and will come again in power and glory to judge both the living and the dead.

We believe in the Holy Spirit, the power of God at work inside of us.

We believe in the church of God, the people of faith throughout the world.

We believe that our sin is forgiven and that we will live together with God for now and throughout eternity.   Amen.

CONFESSION

Lord, God of our tomorrows, we confess our sinful condition before You. We desire something better than what we have and what we are. We know ourselves too well and see our human frailty. We know that our temporary gods are vulnerable and will crumble under the test. We realize that our desires are fickle and backfire on us at the worst times. God of our tomorrows, give us Your forgiveness. Let us see today the promise of something better in our lives.

ABSOLUTION

Our God is a tomorrow God, who knows our past and knows where we are headed. We trust a God who knows our needs and desires each of us to come daily in prayer. As we confess our sins, God is faithful and will forgive our sin and makes us clean from all unrighteousness. God always promises us something better, because of the miracle of forgiveness and love. Praise God from whom all blessings flow.

BENEDICTION

Leader: Go in peace. You are the forgiven people of God.

People: We will celebrate forgiveness in every tomorrow. We will celebrate forgiveness in the week ahead through acts of kindness, times of listening concern, and deeds of generosity.

Leader: Go in peace. You are the forgiven people of God.

People: We have heard the Good News. We will share the Good News.

Leader: The Lord be with you. Go and serve in Jesus' name.

Amen.

CONFESSION

Lord, we come before You in prayer today, asking for forgiveness. We have not loved as we ought to love, we have not given as we ought to give, and we have fallen short of the mark of truly being Your obedient sons and daughters. We recognize our sin and in this moment of silence, we privately remember our shortcomings in love and life. (*Silence for reflection.*)

FORGIVENESS

God, our heavenly Creator, hears the prayers of all people and answers those prayers. Our prayer for forgiveness is answered in the person of Jesus Christ, God's Son, who died for our sin that we might have new life. The distance between God and ourselves has been brought together by love made perfect in the sacrifice of Jesus. To those who believe God's word of turth comes power to be the people of God. Praise God for the gift of love to us.

AFFIRMATION OF FAITH

I believe in a great God who created the world in power and love and whose character is reflected in all of creation.

I believe in Jesus Christ, Son of God and Son of Man. His life, His teachings, His miracles, His death and His resurrection combine to provide true forgiveness of sin and life for all eternity. His strength bolsters my weakness, His love covers my failures and His sacrifice forgives my sin. I trust Him as a friend and brother, a Savior and Lord.

I believe in the Holy Spirit, God at work in and among us. I believe that God is present and active in today's world and that I can know some of the joy of heaven right now. I believe that the church of Christ is the people of God and that in prayer, the sacraments, and the fellowship of the church we can experience true meaning and everlasting love in our lives.

CONFESSION

Lord, our God, we have lived in darkness for too long. We have built walls of isolation so high that the sun no longer is visable. We have a fortress of protection so complete that the sun cannot penetrate. We have stumbled down dark alleys in search of real meaning. God of light and life — illuminate the rooms of our life with your light — and draw us closer to you. Forgive the sin which separates us and allow us to live lives of freedom and acceptance.

A WORD OF HOPE

Our God is Light and in God is real life. Our God has brightened our days with real hope and exposed every dark corner of our life with true forgiveness. The Light of life is Christ Jesus, God's Son, who died on a cross and rose in resurrected glory to give life to a dying world. Through Jesus, we can live in daily relationship with our Creator and know the joy of hope for eternity. Praise God for light and life.

STATEMENT OF FAITH

I believe in a living God, Creator of all humankind, who recreates the entire universe by power and love.

I believe in Jesus Christ, God in the flesh and my Savior and Lord. Because of His work, His death, His life and His suffering, I know who I am and what I can become through Christ.

I believe that God is present with us always and can be experienced in prayer, the Sacraments, the Word, the fellowship of believers and in all that we do.   Amen.

WE CONFESS OUR SIN

Lord, our Spirits are dry. The well that has supplied our ambition and motivation is empty. We are tired of trying to do it alone and acknowledge our need for You. Water of life — Spirit of turth — allow us to drink freely from Your never ending supply of life. We have sinned and we are sorry; we have failed, we need forgiveness; we have searched for love, yet we remain lonely. Fountain of life, You know our needs and our shortcomings — allow us to drink freely from Your never ending supply of life.

A WORD OF GOOD NEWS

Here is the good news! Jesus has come into the world to save sinners. God has not left us alone, but surrounded us with love thorugh the community of believers and filled us with love through the Holy Spirit. God has filled our lives with love until we overflow to those around us. Jesus has given the true gift of love in His death on the cross and His resurrection. Our spirit has been lifted up to new life as the Holy Spirit fills us and lives through us. Praise God for good news!

AFFIRMATION OF FAITH

I believe in God, the Father almighty, creator of heaven and earth.

I believe in Jesus Christ, His only Son, our Lord. He was conceived by the power of the Holy Spirit and born of the virgin Mary. He suffered under Pontius Pilate, was crucified, died, and was buried. He descended into hell. On the third day He rose again. He ascended into heaven, and is seated at the right hand of the Father. He will come again to judge the living and the dead.

I believe in the Holy Spirit, the holy catholic Church, the communion of saints, the forgiveness of sins, the resurrection of the body, and the life everlasting.   Amen.

WE CONFESS OUR SIN

Lord, God of all life, we have tried to build our own world and run it by our own rules. Greed has determined our goals and selfishness has programmed our priorities. The walls we have built around our existence have grown higher and higher so that we no longer see the light of day. God of all life, we desire to see Your world and to live in Your kingdom. Help us to see our sin and turn away from its attraction. Help us to destroy the walls of defensiveness and self-centerdness and build bridges of forgiveness and mutual concern. Your kingdom come, now for us in this life, and the next.

WE HEAR THE GOOD NEWS OF THE KINGDOM

God is the God of all life and created the world out of great love. God's good news for us today is that Jesus' death and resurrection has established a new kingdom, a new place for us to live, a new world of hope and forgiveness where the walls have come down and the bridges are in place. We are free to move about this new kingdom because our sin is forgiven and our lives can be different than they were before. The cross of Christ is the center of this kingdom as we live out our lives in daily struggle with the hard issues of life. The God of all of life loves us with an everlasting love and gives us new power to live our lives with praise and thanksgiving.

AFFIRMATION OF FAITH

We believe in God, the Creator of all things, the source of all goodness and love.

We believe in Jesus Christ, the Son of God, true God yet true man. He was crucified, died and was buried for our sin that we might be free and know the joy of life. He was raised on the third day and ascended to heaven, and will come again in power and glory to judge both the living and the dead.

We believe in the Holy Spirit, the power of God at work inside of us.

We believe in the church of God, the people of faith throughout the world.

We believe that our sin is forgiven and that we will live together with God for now and throughout eternity.   Amen.

WE CONFESS OUR POWERLESSNESS

Lord, we come in worship today admitting that we are powerless to do anything about our sin. Sin separates us from You and our brothers and sisters. Sin ties us up into knots and confuses us. Sin sours our attitudes and destroys right priorities. We are in need of a Savior. We want to live in power and love. We want to know Your power in our lives so that we can be faithful servants in Your world.

WE HEAR THE GOOD NEWS

God created the world out of powerful love and continues to pour out blessings to us. God, in Jesus, went to the cross in powerful love to take the sin of the world to himself so that our sin would no longer weigh us down. God, in the Holy Spirit, continues to demonstrate powerful love as we daily experience God's life-changing power within our lives. Once we were powerless, now we have God's power. Praise God for power to change lives.

AFFIRMATION OF FAITH

We believe in God, the Creator of all things, the source of all goodness and love.

We believe in Jesus Christ, the Son of God, true God yet true man. He was crucified, died and was buried for our sin that we might be free and know the joy of life. He was raised on the third day and ascended to heaven, and will come again in power and glory to judge both the living and the dead.

We believe in the Holy Spirit, the power of God at work inside of us.

We believe in the church of God, the people of faith throughout the world.

We believe that our sin is forgiven and that we will live together with God for now and throughout eternity.   Amen.

WE CONFESS OUR SIN

(A time of silence to remember broken promises, failed relationships, and our separation from the love of God.)

God of Grace, we have sinned, we have missed the mark, we have fallen short of Your expectations for us. Forgive our failures in life and love. Bridge the gaps between us and let us know the true joy of life. We are in need of Good News, God of Grace...we are ready for Your gift...we are thankful for Your grace. Forgive us.

WE HEAR THE GOOD NEWS

Our God of grace has given us the free gift of life in the person of Jesus Christ, true God yet true man, who died on a cruel cross so that our death would lead to eternal life instead of continuous separation. God calls us to live and learn so that our existence can be meaningful. God calls us to forgive and the sins of those around us so that our lives can be lived in harmony with one another. God calls us to watch and pray so that we are in tune with His intent for us and the world. Our God of Grace is a great God. Praise God for love even though we don't deserve it.

AFFIRMATION OF FAITH

I believe in God, the Father almighty, creator of heaven and earth.

I believe in Jesus Christ, His only Son, our Lord. He was conceived by the power of the Holy Spirit and born of the virgin Mary. He suffered under Pontius Pilate, was crucified, died, and was buried. He descended into hell. On the third day He rose again. He ascended into heaven, and is seated at the right hand of the Father. He will come again to judge the living and the dead.

I believe in the Holy Spirit, the holy catholic Church, the communion of saints, the forgiveness of sins, the resurrection of the body, and the life everlasting.   Amen.

WE CONFESS OUR SIN

God of perfect rest, we have run busily from one activity to another, from one posession to another, and from one love to another. We want to be quiet, but we can't. We are distracted by the loud messages of the world calling us to buy and to sell, to build and to boast, and we look for a quiet place of rest. The noise of the traffic drowns out our dissatisfaction, and we move from day to day in a whirl of activity designed to climb the success ladder. We are tired and we need to rest. God of perfect rest, be our resting place, and let us sleep safe in Your arms.

WE HEAR THE GOOD NEWS

Our God, out of love for us, says, "Come to me, all who labor and are heavy laden, and I will give you rest." This promise of God is true. We can rest because our sin is forgiven and our past is forgotten. Jesus loves us with an unconditional love that cuts through our pride and problems to the heart of our needy souls. His death and resurrection provides forgiveness of sin, confidence for today and hope for the future. Praise God for eternal rest.

STATEMENT OF FAITH

We believe in God, who created all that exists and continues to recreate the lives of those who trust. We believe in Jesus Christ, the only Son of a loving God; whose purpose was to save a lost world and who now works in us and others by the Holy Spirit.

We believe that God is calling each of us to be a part of the body of Christ, to celebrate God's presence, to love and serve others, to stand against the powers of injustice and prejudice, and to declare for all the world to hear, "Jesus is risen and we are His people." Thanks be to God.

CONFESSION AND FORGIVENESS

Leader: Let us be honest with ourselves, our God, and with each
         other and confess our sins in order that we might receive
         the forgiveness of God and experience the joy of the commu-
         nity of Christ.

People: Lord, our God, we have sinned by what we have thought,
         said and done. We continue to pull away from You even
         though You love us with an everlasting love. Today in wor-
         ship, we recognize our failures and our weaknesses. We
         confess our sins of omission and commission. We confess
         that we have not loved our neighbor as ourselves. We come
         to You now, as brothers and sisters in Christ, who need
         Your power and forgiveness.

Leader: In the name of Jesus, the Christ, I speak His word to you:
         "I belong to you as you belong to me. I am one of you; I
         know you. I died and rose for you so that your sin might
         be forgiven. I feel what you feel and I live through Your
         life. I forgive your wrongs and with that forgiveness give
         you power to change your condition as you live lives that
         are pleasing in my sight."

AFFIRMATION OF FAITH

I believe in a living God, Creator of all humankind, who recreates
the entire universe by power and love.

I believe in Jesus Christ, God in the flesh and my Savior and Lord.
Because of His work, His death, His life and His suffering, I know
who I am, what I can become through Christ.

I believe that God is present with us always and can be experienced
in prayer, the Sacraments, the Word, the fellowhsip of believers and
in all that we do.   Amen.

CONFESSION

Lord, God of all of our tomorrows, we look back at yesterday and we are sorry. We have not loved as we ought, we have not given ourselves in service to others and we have not responded to Your holy love. We confess that we are powerless to change our condition and that we need Your spirit to lift us up and make our lives right. God of our tomorrows, we need to look forward with hope for our eternity. As we confess our sin to You, forgive us so that we can live forever with You.

WE HEAR THE GOOD NEWS

This is the good news that God sent Jesus into the world that those who believe in Him would have forgiveness of sin and eternal life. We need not fear death....for God is with us. We can place our hope and trust in God because our sin is forgiven and our future is found in the kingdom of heaven. The death and resurrection of Jesus paid the price for our sin and makes this new life possible. Praise God for everlasting love and goodness.

AFFIRMATION OF FAITH

I believe in God, the Father almighty, creator of heaven and earth.

I believe in Jesus Christ, His only Son, our Lord. He was conceived by the power of the Holy Spirit and born of the virgin Mary. He suffered under Pontius Pilate, was crucified, died, and was buried. He descended into hell. On the third day He rose again. He ascended into heaven, and is seated at the right hand of the Father. He will come again to judge the living and the dead.

I believe in the Holy Spirit, the holy catholic Church, the communion of saints, the forgiveness of sins, the resurrection of the body, and the life everlasting.   Amen.

CONFESSION

Our hearts seem heavy, Lord, because we carry the weight of our past with us. We have not forgotten about our yesterdays and the memories of our past threaten to undo us. We are tired and we need to rest. We have walked for too long on our own and we need a Savior to carry our sin. God of compassion, lift the burden of our sin and forgive us so that we can be freed up to live new lives in You.

WE HEAR THE GOOD NEWS

Your God is a God of compassion and has heard your voices asking for forgiveness. You no longer need to carry the weight of your own sin because it has been lifted from you and taken to the Cross with Jesus, the true Son of God. The sin which seemed so heavy is forgiven. You are free, you can stand straight and walk confident in the love and care of you Creator. Praise God!

AFFIRMATION OF FAITH

I believe in a living God, Creator of all humankind, who recreates the entire universe by power and love.

I believe in Jesus Christ, God in the flesh and my Savior and Lord. Because of His work, His death, His life and His suffering, I know who I am, what I can become through Christ.

I believe that God is present with us always and can be experienced in prayer, the Sacraments, the Word, the fellowhsip of believers and in all that we do.   Amen.

CONFESSION

Lord, God of grace and glory, we come to You today as family members who have sinned and fallen short. We have not given ourselves in love and service. We have followed our own selfish desires, ignoring the needs of the community of faith around us. Forgive our sin, sensitize us to the brothers and sisters who need our concern and give us faith and power for today.

WE HEAR THE GOOD NEWS

God has shown grace and glory to us. Jesus, God's Son, went to the cross to pay the price for our sin and separation in order that we would be made right and could be part of the family again. Through the Holy Spirit we are given power to change and become new each day as God lives life through us. We share in the death of Jesus just as we share His resurrection. We have been made one with the family of God again. Praise God for grace and glory.

NICENE CREED

We believe in one God, the Father, the Almighty, maker of heaven and earth, of all that is, seen and unseen.

We believe in one Lord, Jesus Christ, the only Son of God, eternally begotten of the Father, God from God, Light from Light, true God from true God, begotten, not made, of one Being with the Father. Through Him all things were made. For us and for our salvation He came down from heaven; by the power of the Holy Spirit He became incarnate from the virgin Mary, and was made man. For our sake He was crucified under Pontius Pilate; He suffered death and was buried. On the third day He rose again in accordance with the Scriptures; He ascended into heaven and is seated at the right hand of the Father. He will come again in glory to judge the living and the dead, and His kingdom will have no end.

We believe in the Holy Spirit, the Lord, the giver of life, who proceeds from the Father and the Son. With the Father and the Son He is worshiped and glorified. He has spoken through the prophets. We believe in one holy catholic and apostolic Chruch. We acknowledge one Baptism for the forgiveness of sins. We look for the resurrection of the dead, and the life of the world to come.   Amen.

A CELEBRATION
OF DAILY BREAD (Communion)

WE CONFESS OUR SIN (together)

Lord, we confess our sin. You have promised to provide for all of our needs, and yet we mistrust Your promise. We know the futility of our own ambitions and our inability to do that which we desire. Today we need to recognize the sin within us, and ask that you would forgive us. Lord, in Your mercy, give us daily bread, not only for our bodies, but as food for our spirits. Forgive our sin and cleanse us so that we can be pleasing in Your sight and ministers in Your service.

WE HEAR THE GOOD NEWS

Our God is a great God, providing for all of our needs, giving us daily bread and supplies for every spiritual need. Our sin no longer controls us. Our response to God's love is the focus for our lives. The death of Jesus Christ has paid the cost of our sin and has set us free to live in victory. We are forgiven. We are daughters and sons of God. We are ministers to each other. Praise God for the daily provision for our every need.

AFFIRMATION OF FAITH

I believe in God, who has created all things and continues to create new life within us.

I believe in Jesus, son of God, son of man, the Savior of the world. By His life, His death and resurrection, I can know the true depth of human possibility, and experience the true joy of an abundant life.

I believe that the Holy Spirit is present, now and always, calling us to faith, giving us gifts and empowering us for service.

I believe that the community of believers called the church can experience the fulness of life through the word, the sacraments, and all that we do.

COMMUNION LITURGY

The Invitation

Leader: Welcome to the celebration! God who supplies our every
          need has given us this meal to share.
People: Lord, we thank You for the bread of eternal life.
Leader: We come to the table, acknowledging our shortcomings
          and our need to experience Your presence in bread and wine.
People: Lord, we thank You for the bread of eternal life.

CONFESSION

Lord, today we recognize our lack of faith. We have not kept our eyes on You and we have been distracted by the sights around us. We have been listening to other voices which beg us to crawl inward and self destruct. Today, as we hear Your call to "come," give us faith so we need not be afraid. Forgive our failures in love and life. Forgive our sin.

ABSOLUTION

Today we can celebrate faith because our God gives us faith for every purpose and strength for every need. Our God sent Jesus to the cross to die in our place so that our lives could have eternal value. Our God has forgiven our sin through Jesus and our response to that love is lives that are ground in faith and powered by service. Our faith is a gift; our life is a gift; our eternal life is a gift of our loving God. Praise God for the gift of faith.

NICENE CREED

We believe in one God, the Father, the Almighty, maker of heaven and earth, of all that is, seen and unseen.

We believe in one Lord, Jesus Christ, the only Son of God, eternally begotten of the Father, God from God, Light from Light, true God from ture God, begotten, not made, of one Being with the Father. Through Him all things were made. For us and for our salvation He came down from heaven; by the power of the Holy Spirit He became incarnate from the virgin Mary, and was made man. For our sake He was crucified under Pontius Pilate; He suffered death and was buried. On the third day He rose again in accordance with the Scriptures; He ascended into heaven and is seated at the right hand of the Father. He will come again in glory to judge the living and the dead, and His kingdom will have no end.

We believe in the Holy Spirit, the Lord, the giver of life, who proceeds from the Father and the Son. With the Father and the Son He is worshiped and glorified. He has spoken through the prophets. We believe in one holy catholic and apostolic Church. We acknowledge one Baptism for the forgiveness of sins. We look for the resurrection of the dead, and the life of the world to come.   Amen.

COMMUNION LITURGY

Leader: We declare ourselves to be the Easter Community.

People: We are here because Jesus is the Good News for all people.

Leader: He took the sad news of our sin and guilt and turned it around through His dying for it and raising for us.

People: Now, we are a part of that new people in Christ, and come here to celebrate His Resurrection and presence.

Leader: Jesus was broken for us and torn apart for us to be healed.

People: He rose from the grave to unleash new life in the world.

Leader: And He took the bread, blessed it, and broke it. He said to His friends, "Take, eat; this is my body."

People: Also, He took a cup, filled with fruit of the vine. After thanks, He gave it to them saying, "Drink of it, all of you; for this is my blood of the covenant."

PRAYER OF THANKSGIVING:

Our living Master, take us as unworthy as we are, into the fellowship of Your redemeed. We acknowledge our shortcomings and our sins, our inconsistent minds and hearts, and our slackness of devotion. But You do not forsake us even when we betray You. So accept us not for what we are, but for what You can create in us. We thank You that our individual lives can be more complete as we live in communion with You, O Christ, and with others. In Your Spirit.   Amen.

CONFESSION

Lord, we come before You in prayer today, asking for forgiveness. We have not loved as we ought to love, we have not given as we ought to give, and we have fallen short of the mark of truly being Your obedient sons and daughters. We recognize our sin and in this moment of silence, we privately remember our shortcomings in love and life. (*silence for reflection*)

WE HEAR THE GOOD NEWS

God, our heavenly love, hears the prayers of all children and answers those prayers. Our prayer for forgiveness is answered in the person of Jesus Christ, God's Son, who died for our sin that we might have new life. The distance between God and ourselves has been brought together by love made perfect in the sacrifice of Jesus. To those who believe God's word of truth comes the power to be the people of God. Praise God for the gift of love to us.

NICENE CREED

We believe in one God, the Father, the Almighty, maker of heaven and earth, of all that is, seen and unseen.

We believe in one Lord, Jesus Christ, the only Son of God, eternally begotten of the Father, God from God, Light from Light, true God from true God, begotten, not made, of one Being with the Father. Through Him all things were made. For us and for our salvation He came down from heaven; by the power of the Holy Spirit He became incarnate from the virgin Mary, and was made man. For our sake He was crucified under Pontius Pilate; He suffered death and was buried. On the third day He rose again in accordance with the Scriptures; He ascended into heaven and is seated at the right hand of the Father. He will come again in glory to judge the living and the dead, and His kingdom will have no end.

We believe in the Holy Spirit, the Lord, the giver of life, who proceeds from the Father and the Son. With the Father and the Son He is worshiped and glorified. He has spoken through the prophets. We believe in one holy catholic and apostolic Church. We acknowledge one Baptism for the forgiveness of sins. We look for the resurrection of the dead, and the life of the world to come. Amen.

THE COMMUNION

Leader: We declare ourselves to be Easter people.

People: We have come to share in the table that Jesus has prepared for us.

Leader: He took the bad news of sin and guilt and changed it to good news through His dying and rising for us.

People: We are here to celebrate that Good News and the presence of Christ with us.

Leader: And He took the bread, blessed it, and broke it. He said to His disciples;

People: "Take, eat; this is my body."

Leader: Also, He took a cup of wine. After saying thanks, He gave it to them saying:

People: "Drink of it, all of you for this is my blood of the covenant. It is poured out for the forgiveness of sins. Do this to remember me."

Leader: We thank You, Lord God, for these elements given in love for us. Accept us, forgive us, and heal us, that we might live lives that are pleasing to You.

AFFIRMATION OF FAITH

We believe in one God, the Father, the Almighty, maker of heaven and earth, of all that is, seen and unseen.

We believe in one Lord, Jesus Christ, the only Son of God, eternally begotten of the Father, God from God, Light from Light, true God from true God, begotten, not made, of one Being with the Father. Through Him all things were made. For us and for our salvation He came down from heaven; by the power of the Holy Spirit He became incarnate from the virgin Mary, and was made man. For our sake He was crucified under Pontius Pilate; He suffered death and was buried. On the third day He rose again in accordance with the Scriptures; He ascended into heaven and is seated at the right hand of the Father. He will come again in glory to judge the living and the dead, and His kingdom will have no end.

We believe in the Holy Spirit, the Lord, the giver of life, who proceeds from the Father and the Son. With the Father and the Son He is worshiped and glorified. He has spoken through the prophets. We believe in one holy catholic and apostolic Chruch. We acknowledge one Baptism for the forgiveness of sins. We look for the resurrection of the dead, and the life of the world to come.

Amen.

COMMUNION LITURGY

Leader: We declare ourselves to be Easter people.

People: We have come to share in the table that He has prepared for us.

Leader: He took the bad news of sin and guilt and changed it to good news through His dying and rising for us.

People: We are here to celebrate that Good News and the presence of Christ with us.

Leader: And He took the break, blessed it, and broke it. He said to His disciples:

People: "Take, eat; this is my body."

Leader: Also, He took a cup of wine. After saying thanks, He gave it to them saying:

People: "Drink of it, all of you for this is my blood of the covenant. It is poured out for the forgiveness of sins. Do this to remember me."

Leader: We thank You, Lord God, for these elements given in love for us. Accept us, forgive us, and heal us, that we might live lives that are pleasing to You.

WE CONFESS OUR BROKENNESS

Lord, we have sinned and fallen short of the mark. We have pulled away and charted our own course. We have heard Your call, but we have not responded as we ought. We have searched everywhere for loving arms and caring words, but we have only found confusion and discontent. We would like to change and be different, but we know our limitations. God of our tomorrows, forgive our sin and make life right again.

WE HEAR OF OUR HEALING

Our God is a God of comfort and healing. Our God has extended the hand of unconditional love and offers to hold us in loving arms for all eternity. Our God, in Jesus, had hands nailed to a cross in order that we could know the joy of life and live together. Jesus' hands of love continue to beckon us daily, calling for us to follow and serve. The resurrected and ascended Jesus offers healing for our bodies and our spirits. Praise God for the gift of new life.

COMMUNION LITURGY

Leader: We declare ourselves to be Easter people.

People: We have come to share in the table that He has prepared for us.

Leader: He took the bad news of sin and guilt and changed it to good news through His dying and rising for us.

People: We are here to celebrate that Good News and the presence of Christ with us.

Leader: And He took the break, blessed it, and broke it. He said to His disciples:

People: "Take, eat; this is my body."

Leader: Also, He took a cup of wine. After saying thanks, He gave it to them saying:

People: "Drink of it, all of you for this is my blood of the covenant. It is poured out for the forgiveness of sins. Do this to remember me."

Leader: We thank You, Lord God, for these elements given in love for us. Accept us, forgive us, and heal us, that we might live lives that are pleasing to You.

A CELEBRATION OF GIFTS — FINE ARTS SUNDAY

The focus of the service today is the gifts and talents which bless our congregation. The special music, the readers, the artwork and crafts which decorate the church all serve to celebrate the many gifts of God. We are thankful for His rich blessings that today we celebrate.

PRELUDE
OPENING HYMN
OPENING PRAYER
WELCOME TO WORSHIP
(Worshippers will turn and greet each other being sure to exchange names and a little about each other.)

HYMN
CONFESSION — Our Use of the Gifts

Leader: In the name of the Creator, the Christ and Holy Spirit.
People: Amen.
Leader: We are here as the celebrating church, unashamed in our joy and again willing to be touched by the Gift of Life from God.
People: Into our nostril God blew the breath of life.
Leader: And we became a living being.
People: Amen.
Leader: We have been given great gifts by our Creator — gifts for teaching, healing, and helping.
People: But we have not used the gifts as we ought. We instead choose to love the trinkets of the world, even though they rust in our hands.
Leader: We have been given talents and abilities for the betterment of the Realm of God on this earth.
People: But we have chosen to build our own private kingdoms hidden walls of fear and greed. Lord, forgive our neglected vows, our broken promises, and the sin which separates us from you.

ABSOLUTION — The Giver of the Gifts

Leader: Today is an amazing day! This is the day which the Lord has made and we come as children of God to give thanks for goodness to us. God has forgiven our sin, made good on our broken promises and fulfilled our neglected vows in death on the cross and the gift of eternal life in the resurrection. We are free because of great love for us. We are free to discover God's gifts and use them in service to others. We are free to live life to the fullest. We are free to love one another with a new kind of love.

HYMN OF PRAISE

SCRIPTURE LESSONS ON THE USE OF THE GIFTS

TIME OF SPECIAL MUSIC

(A time of sharing for persons with vocal or instrumental ability to offer music as a special offering to God.)

AFFIRMATION OF FAITH

We believe in God, who created and is creating. God came to earth in human form — Jesus — to save a troubled world from sin and death and give us the possibility of eternal life. We believe that the Holy Spirit is God with us — working in and through us to make all things new and give hope where there is despair.

God calls each of us to discipleship...to belong...to reach out and to care. God calls us to be kind to others, to work for justice on earth and to feed and clothe the poor and the hungry. God asks each of us to publicly proclaim Jesus as the Messiah, the Savior of the World.

OFFERTORY
SPECIAL MUSIC
PASTORAL PRAYERS
SERMON
BENEDICTION
CLOSING HYMN
POSTLUDE

ORDER OF WORSHIP FOR MAUNDY THURSDAY

Maundy is an English form of the Latin word for *commandment man-datum*, the new commandment to "love one another as I have loved you."

PRELUDE
OPENING HYMN
THE GREETING

Leader: We have come in the Name of the God who created us, in the name of the Son who has given us new life, and in the name of the Spirit that brings unity and oneness.

People: Let us worship God, the Creator, Son, and Holy Spirit. May our love for one another be a reflection of the true love of God in Jesus Christ.

THE TIME OF CONFESSION
(Silent time — the entire period of Lent is a time for reflection and confession beginning with Ash Wednesday — the emphasis of Holy Thursday is the ending of the time of confession and focusing on forgiveness.)

THE WORDS OF FORGIVENESS
   Colossians 1:14
   Romans 5:1
   Galatians 2:20
   Ephesians 1:7
LENTEN HYMN
SCRIPTURE LESSONS FOR THE EVENING
HYMN
THE SERMON
OFFERTORY
SPECIAL MUSIC
THE PRESENTATION OF THE GIFTS
(The bread, wine and offering gifts are brought forward to the altar at this time.)

PRAYER FOR THE GIFTS

Each day is our new beginning. Help us to remember that you have given us this day to make of it as we will. This is a day to be filled with love and service to others. This is a day to remember Your love and mercy that comes fresh every morning and carries us through the difficult times of the day. Receive these gifts from our time and our possessions. May they be a simple token of our overflowing love for you and the world around us.   Amen.

THE WORDS OF INSTITUTION

THE LORD'S PRAYER

THE DISTRIBUTION

POST COMMUNION PRAYER

We give thanks, Lord, that You have brought refreshment with these elements and given us the gift of life. We pray that we would be strengthened by this gift — in faith toward you and in love for each other. In the name of Jesus Christ, our Lord.   Amen.

THE STRIPPING OF THE ALTAR

(The altar represents Christ and the removal of the vessels is symbolic of the humiliation of Christ. A Scripture passage is read as each is removed and processed down center aisle.)

Psalm 22:1-5   The Removal of the Bread and Wine
Psalm 22:24-30   The Removal of the Altar Candles
Psalm 20:1-4   The Removal of the Missal Stand and Altar Books
Psalm 20   The Removal of the Banners and Paraments

THE ENTRANCE OF THE CROWN OF THORNS

(In silence a crown of thorns is processed and placed on the altar — there is a time of silent meditation and then the congregation can leave in quiet.)

ORDER OF WORSHIP
FOR GOOD FRIDAY

MEDITATION BEFORE
THE WORSHIP

The word *Tenebrae* means "darkness." In this service as each scripture is read, one candle is extinguished. The increasing darkness also symbolizes the flight and denial of the disciples and friends of Jesus. The moment of darkness recalls the death of Christ. The veiling of the cross combined with the crown of thorns and the darkness symbolizes our mourning over our sin and the sins of the world. In this darkness there is but one light — the eternal light of Christ. Even though darkness settled upon the earth, the light of God reminds us of the never failing presence of God's forgiveness and grace.

PRELUDE

OPENING HYMN   "O Sacred Head Now Wounded"

PRAYER OF CONFESSION

Leader: Dear God, this night is filled with darkenss and mourning, but we need to remember. Help us to remember.

People: We need to remember that we are Your creation and that we are created in Your image and reflections of Your love.

Leader: We remember yesterday and we are sorry because we have failed in love and friendship. We have tried so hard but we have failed so miserably.

People: On this night of darkness, may Your presence remove our sorrow and fill us with a new sense of purpose and fulfillment.   Amen.

THE SCRIPTURE LESSON FOR THE EVENING
John 19:17-30

SILENT MEDITATION
AND CANDLE LIGHTING
(*A time for silent reflection and meditation on the significance of this night. As the candles are lit, the lights in the room are diminished until only the light of the candles is evident.*)

THE SERMON

OFFERTORY
(*A procession of the congregation to the altar with the gifts.*)
SPECIAL MUSIC
(*during the offertory*)

THE PROCESSION OF THE CROSS

(*A large wooden cross is processed down the center aisle and placed in the front of the church, leaning on the altar, or in its own stand.*)

HYMN DURING THE PROCESSION
"Beneath the Cross of Jesus"

READINGS FROM THE CROSS

(*As each lesson is read one candle is extinguished until only a light on the cross remains.*)
1. The Darkness of Betrayal   Matthew 26:20-25
2. The Darkness of Desertion   Matthew 26:47-56
3. The Dark Agony of the Spirit   Matthew 27:11-26
4. The Darkness of Misunderstanding   Mark 14:3-8
5. The Darkness of Broken Trust   John 16:29-32
6. The Darkenss of Death   John 19:25-30
7. The Darkenss of the Cross   John 19:31-42

The congregation may sit quietly and meditate and when ready to leave may leave in silence preparing for the good news of Easter.

WE GATHER IN DARKNESS

The Procession of the Thorns (*The thorns placed on the later on Maundy Thursday, and processed down the center aisle in silence.*)

WE HEAR THE GOOD NEWS

(*A reader from in the congregation stands up and reads.*)

Now after the Sabbath, toward the dawn of the first day of the week, Mary Magdalene and the other Mary went to see the tomb. And behold, there was a great earthquake; for an angel of the Lord descended from heaven and came and rolled back the stone and sat upon it. His appearance was like lightning, and his rainment white as snow. And for fear of him the guards trembled and became like dead men. But the angel said to the women, "Do not be afraid; for I know that you seek Jesus who was crucified. He is not here; for He has risen, as He said. Come, see the place where He lay. Then go tell His disciples that He has risen from the dead, and behold, He is going before you to Galilee; there you will see Him."

TRUMPET FANFARE

(*A loud trumpet heralds the good news and the resurrection of the Lord.*)

EASTER HYMN   "Jesus Christ Is Risen Today"

THE WELCOME

(*Each worshipper turns and greets those standing nearby with the words "Good Morning — He Is Risen."*)

THE LITANY FOR EASTER MORNING

Leader: People of God, you have come seeking the Christ, the Son of the living God.

People: Yes, we have set our doubts aside and we have come. We have lived with our fear too long and we have come. We have heard that Jesus has conquered death and we want to hear that good news again.

Leader: Do not be afraid, for He has risen from the dead, He has broken the tomb wide open, He has come back to life and is living together with us right here — right now.

People: We have felt His lonliness, we have prayed His prayers, and we have deserted Him. We feel guilty.

Leader: There is no need for your guilt — for He has taken it with Him to the cross and has paid the ultimate price for your sin. This is good news — He is alive — so that we can be alive.

People: This is good news — He is alive.

Leader: He has risen!

People: He has risen!

Prayer of the Community

God of great wonder, we sense the greatness of today and we feel like shouting from the rooftops. Our pain has been turned to joy, our guilt has been turned to happiness and our despair has been turned to hope. We thank you that Jesus is with us and that His presence breaks through the silence of this morning. Your perfect plan is complete and we give you thanks and praise for this Easter day.   Amen.

Special Music
Scripture Readings for the Day

Affirmation of Faith

I believe in a great God who created the world in power and love and whose character is reflected in all of creation.

I believe in Jesus Christ, Son of God and Son of Man. His life, His teachings, His miracles, His death and His resurrection combine to provide true forgiveness of sin and life for all eternity. His strength bolsters my weakness, His love covers my failures and His sacrifice forgives my sin. I trust Him as a friend and brother, a Savior and Lord.

I believe in the Holy Spirit, God at work in and among us. I believe that God is present and active in today's world and that I can know some of the joy of heaven right now. I believe that the church of Christ is the people of God and that in prayer, the sacraments, and the fellowship of the church we can experience true meaning and everlasting love in our lives.

Offerings and Announcements
Easter Hymn
The Easter Message
Benediction
Closing Hymn
"Christ Is Alive, Let Christians Sing"
Postlude

PRELUDE

THE CALL TO WORSHIP — **Brass Choir**

PROCESSIONAL AND OPENING HYMN
— "Jesus Christ Is Risen Today"

WELCOME TO WORSHIP
(Worshippers greet one another by moving about, shaking hands, introducing each other, and saying "He Is Risen!" or "Happy Easter.")

LITANY FOR EASTER

Leader: In the Name of God, our Creator, in the name of Jesus, our Savior, and in the name of the Spirit, our comforter, we have come to worship the Lord. Amen.

People: We are the Easter people who have been to the tomb and proclaim that it is empty indeed. He is Risen!

Leader: He is Risen, indeed!

People: We are the Easter people who have met Him by the roadside and recognized Him as the Son of God — risen from the dead — and living in this world and the next. He is Risen!

Leader: He is Risen indeed!

People: We are the Easter people who have placed our hand in His side and felt His wounds. He was once dead but is now alive. He has been raised by the triumphant power of the Almighty God...He is Risen!

Leader: He is risen, indeed! We worship a Risen Lord.

EASTER HYMN

CONFESSION

God of Easter, and God of Good Friday, we see in Your death the good news of our own Resurrection. We have felt the despair of our own Good Fridays, wondering if Easter would ever come. We need to be resurrected, Lord. We need the promise of new life and the hope of conquered death. On this Easter morning, break through the barriers of our sin and shame and bring your peace to our troubled hearts.

WE HEAR THE GOOD NEWS

Today brings the best news of all...Jesus lives! Jesus died on the cross — a cruel death — for the sin of the whole world. He was placed in a borrowed tomb and on the third day — came back to life to defeat death for all time and offer to us this new life as our very own. Our sin is forgiven because Jesus lives. We no longer need to fear death as we look forward to living for all eternity with Him. Jesus lives! Praise God for the good news of Easter.

EASTER HYMN
SCRIPTURE LESSONS (read the Easter texts)
SPECIAL MUSIC
(*Anyone in the congregation who has ever performed the "Hallelujah Chorus" should join the choir in the choir loft and in mass chorus sing this all-time favorite.*)

"Hallelujah Chorus"   Handel

AFFIRMATION OF FAITH

We believe in one God, the Father, the Almighty, maker of heaven and earth, of all that is, seen and unseen.

We believe in one Lord, Jesus Christ, the only Son of God, eternally begotten of the Father, God from God, Light from Light, true God from true God, begotten, not made, of one Being with the Father. Through Him all things were made. For us and for our salvation He came down from heaven; by the power of the Holy Spirit He became incarnate from the virgin Mary, and was made man. For our sake He was crucified under Pontius Pilate; He suffered death and was buried. On the third day He rose again in accordance with the Scriptures; He ascended into heaven and is seated at the right hand of the Father. He will come again in glory to judge the living and the dead, and His kingdom will have no end.

We believe in the Holy Spirit, the Lord, the giver of life, who proceeds from the Father and the Son. With the Father and the Son He is worshiped and glorified. He has spoken through the prophets. We believe in one holy catholic and apostolic Church. We acknowledge one Baptism for the forgiveness of sins. We look for the resurrection of the dead, and the life of the world to come. Amen.

OFFERTORY
SPECIAL MUSIC
PASTORAL PRAYERS
SERMON
BENEDICTION
CLOSING HYMN
POSTLUDE

PRELUDE
OPENING HYMN
OPENING PRAYER
WELCOME TO WORSHIP
(*The worshippers spend several minutes greeting one another.*)

LITANY FOR PENTECOST

Leader: We have come to worship in spirit and truth.
People: God is with us...God lives.
Leader: We have come to share the Good News.
People: The Spirit of God is moving among us, calling us, leading us, strengthening us.
Leader: We have come to confirm the activity of the Spirit of God.
People: God is at work, among and within, in our world and the next...in us and those around us...to make all things new and recreate life in all the people of God.

PENTECOST HYMN

Acts 2:1-4   When the day of Pentecost came, all the believers were gathered together in one place. Suddenly there was a noise from the sky which sounded like a strong wind blowing, and it filled the whole house where they were sitting. Then they saw what looked like tongues of fire which spread out and touched each person there. They were all filled with the Holy Spirit and began to talk in other languages.

HYMN OF PRAISE

VERSES ABOUT THE SPIRIT

Matthew 3:11   (John the Baptist speaking)
        "I baptize you with water for repentance, but he who is coming after me is mightier than I, whose sandals I am not worthy to carry; he will baptize you with the Holy Spirit and with fire."
John 20:22   (Jesus speaking to His disciples)
        "Peace be with you. As the Father has sent me, even so I send you. And when he had said this, he breathed on them, and said to them, 'Receive the Holy Spirit.' If you forgive the sins of any, they are forgiven; if you retain the sins of any they are retained."

John 3:5

"Truly I say to you, unless one is born of water and the Spirit, he cannot enter the Kingdom of God. That which is born of the flesh is flesh and that which is born of the Spirit is spirit."

John 14:26

"But the Counselor, the Holy Spirit, whom the Father will send in my name, He will teach you all things, and bring to your remembrance all that I have said to you. Peace I leave with you; my peace I give to you."

1 Corinthians 3:16

"Do you not know that you are God's temple and that God's spirit dwells in you."

1 Corinthians 12:4

"Now there are varieties of gifts, but the same spirit. For by one Spirit we were all baptized into one obeyed — Jews or Greeks, slaves or free and all were made to drink of one Spirit.

SPECIAL MUSIC

CONFESSION

God of spirit and truth...we come in worship to confess that we are sinful and unclean. Our spirits are dry and we need to be refreshed by Your Spirit. We have tried to live life on our own terms but have failed. Our days run together and we lack adventure and motivation in our lives. God of spirit and truth...forgive our sin and refresh us with Your Spirit.

ABSOLUTION

I believe that God is real and that the world was created with me in mind. I believe that I am loved by a loving God who knows all about me and is prepared to meet my every need.

I believe in Jesus of Nazareth, the son of a carpenter, born to Mary through a miracle of God. I believe that Jesus is true God and true man at the same time and that this Jesus is God's method for providing for the saving of a lost world. I believe that Jesus lived, died, and was resurrected to pay the price for my sin and that I will live together with Him for all eternity.

I believe that God lives with me through the Holy Spirit. I believe that the Holy Spirit calls me in to true faith, sustains me in times of great despair and leads me into the true knowledge of Jesus as the Way, Truth, and Life. I believe that the Holy Spirit has given me gifts to use within the body of Christ and that these gifts bring completeness as we gather together in worship and service.

PRELUDE
ANNOUNCEMENTS
OPENING HYMN
WELCOME TO WORSHIP
(*Worshippers turn to one another and greet each other. Take several minutes.*)

THE LITANY FOR THANKSGIVING

Leader: Welcome to the Celebration. Welcome to the worship. We have come together to give thanks and offer praise.
People: We are the people of God — gathered here in this place to give thanks for the many blessings that we enjoy every day.
Leader: We have come together to worship God, our Creator, the giver of every gift, the source of every blessing.
People: We will lift our voices in song, we will listen to the good news, and we will respond to the love of God.
Leader: Welcome to the celebration.

THANKSGIVING HYMN

CONFESSION

We confess that we have not loved our God or our neighbor as ourselves. We have not given thanks with our hearts, our minds, and our voices. We have failed to recognize the great things that God has done through countless gifts of love. We have come to give thanks, but we first need to confess our sin. Our failures are very real and our feelings of discouragement continue to haunt us. Lord, God of all of us, forgive our sin. See through our failures and disappointments to the hearts of people who desire only to serve You in a troubled world.

ABSOLUTION

God hears our prayer for forgiveness and has forgiven our sin in the person of Jesus Christ. Where we have failed, God has triumphed. Where we have fallen short, God has won the prize. Our sin is forgiven and this is the Good News...that we are no longer slaves to our former selves but have been freed up to be the real people of God. We can worship our God with a new sense of what Thanksgiving really means. Praise God for wonderful love.

THANKSGIVING HYMN
SCRIPTURE READINGS FOR THANKSGIVING
APOSTLES' CREED
OFFERTORY
SPECIAL MUSIC
THE PRAYERS
THE SERMON
THE BENEDICTION
CLOSING HYMN
POSTLUDE

PRELUDE
OPENING HYMN

THE CALL TO WORSHIP

Leader: Glory to God in the highest.
People: And on earth peace, good will toward everyone.
Leader: Behold, I bring you good tidings of great joy, which will
         come to all people.
People: Glory be to God on high.
Leader: For to you is born this day, in the city of David, a Savior,
         who is Christ the Lord.
People: Glory to God in the highest, and on earth peace, good
         will to everyone.

WELCOME TO WORSHIP(*The worshippers will move about and
greet each other with a hearty "Merry Christmas."*)

THE INVOCATION

We thank you, O God, for the songs of that first Christmas which
were sung by the angelic chorus. As their words removed fear from
the shepherds, and pronounced to them the good news that Christ
was born, we ask, too, that our troubled hearts would find calm and
contentment in the still of this Christmas night. In the name of the
Christ Child, born to a broken world for forgiveness' sake.   Amen.

CHRISTMAS HYMN

THE LITANY OF WORD AND SONG

Leader: Make a joyful noise unto the Lord, all the earth; break forth and sing for joy. Joy to the world the Lord is come. Break forth and sing...for joy.

People: (*Singing*)
Joy to the world, the Lord is come
Let earth receive her king
Let every hearty prepare Him room
And heaven and nature sing

Leader: Sing to the Lord, all the world. Worship the Lord with joy; come before Him with happy songs. Never forget that the Lod is God. He made us and we belong to Him. We are His people and the sheep of His pasture.

People: (*Singing*)
Joy to the world the Savior reigns
Let men their songs employ
While fields and floods, rocks, hills, and plains
Repeat the sounding joy

Leader: Sing a new song to the Lord for He has done wonderful things! By His own power and holy strength He has won the victory. The Lord has announced His victory; He made His saving power known to the nations.

People: (*Singing*)
He rules the world with truth and grace
And makes the nations prove
The glories of His righteousness
And wonders of His love

THE HOLY FAMILY
(*A family from the congregation, with a samll baby enters, dressed as Mary and Joseph and the baby Jesus and is seated at the front of the Sanctuary.*)

CHRISTMAS CAROLS
THE CHRISTMAS STORY
(*Read by Joseph*)   Luke 2:1-20
SPECIAL MUSIC
(*Holy family exits*)
OFFERTORY
HYMN BEFORE THE SERMON
PASTORAL PRAYERS
SERMON
BENEDICTION
CLOSING HYMN
POSTLUDE

G

H

I

J

INDEX

HYMN USAGE INDEX

Below is an index with suggested usage of some of the hymns in the book. Obviously, some hymns are suitable for many occasions and can be used throughout the year. When selecting hymns not only be aware of the text and message but the pace and mood of the song for the particular place in the service. Be creative.

HYMN USAGE INDEX

FOR FURTHER INFORMATION

A videotape has been prepared by Handt Hanson explaining the use of this hymnal and the part that it can play in contemporary worship. Portions of actual contemporary worship services are included. For information on this and other products available from Prince of Peace Publishing, please write or call:

Prince of Peace Publishing
13801 Fairview Drive
Burnsville, MN 55337
(612) 435-8107